The Ascending Leader

Conquer the
Seven Enemies of Success—
A Strategic Guide
for the Newly Promoted

By Diane Egbers and Karen Schenck

A Smart Business Network Inc. imprint

For information and inquiries, address

Smart Business Network
835 Sharon Drive,
Westlake, OH 44145,
or call (800) 988-4726.

Cover design by Stacy Vickroy/Amanda Horvath
Layout and design by Kaelyn Hrabak and Randy Wood
Edited by Randy Wood
Photos courtesy of Google Images

ISBN: 978-0-9889622-0-0

Library of Congress Control Number: 2013933085

Dedication

To Tom with all my love, along with Grant and Olivia who are the joy of my life and constant source of inspiration.

To Mom and Dad with gratitude for your faith and unconditional love.

To our extended families, I am so richly blessed by each of you.

D.E.

To Tom, My Beautiful Man and the Love of My Life, who makes life a grand adventure.

To my step-children and grandchildren, who are a constant source of joy.

To my parents and family, for a lifetime of love and support.

K.S.

Contents

Foreword

In June 2010, we were conducting our formal senior leadership talent review. Gathered were our most senior executives dedicated to discussing our high potentials across the company's footprint. This session was a major milestone in our talent review cycle, through which over 2,500 leaders were discussed and assessed on their performance and potential.

The discussions during these two days were insightful, candid and constructive. Our executives were openly and sincerely acknowledging leaders not only for their business performance, but also for their leadership competencies and emotional intelligence. They were problem solving – How do we get Sandra and Bill ready for their next positions? What experiences, special projects, leadership initiatives and short-term assignments do they need in order to expedite their career development? I remember thinking how far our talent reviews had come. These were exactly the type of conversations we need to have to maintain and grow our talent pipeline. But there was one discussion that concerned me.

We began talking about Mitch (alias), who had been promoted to run a line of business in one of our markets nine months prior. Mitch had been "on the radar" for promotion two years running before this opportunity arose. He had been seen as not only being ready for this position, but also having a long runway for future positions in the company. Our discussion, however, highlighted challenges he was currently experiencing. Mitch wasn't doing as well as expected. By the end of the talent discussion, there were seeds of doubt as to whether we had made the right move. We questioned whether Mitch could meet our expectations in a reasonable time frame.

While this example wouldn't surprise any readers who have been a part of talent discussions, it still concerned me. How did this happen? How could a top-box leader be struggling? Was it a tougher market? Did he have the right players on his team? Were there personal or external contributing factors? What was keeping him from performing as he had before? Did we move him too soon? After follow-up dialogue with a few of the participating senior leaders, I discovered I wasn't the only one who was curious about this. Subsequent conversations with other leaders confirmed we had to do something about it. After all, Mitch wasn't the only leader who had been challenged by a new job and associated performance expectations. We needed to make certain our leaders had every opportunity to succeed in their new roles.

Motivated by the vision of Greg Love, Director of Coaching and Development for the company, we enlisted the partnership of Diane Egbers, Karen Schenck and Matt Marvin with Leadership Excelleration, Inc. (LEI Consulting). Together, we customized and delivered the Leader Assimilation Program. It was created to aid operational and strategic leaders in effectively transitioning into their new roles, whether they were internally promoted or externally hired. The Program is structured, yet is flexible enough to adapt to each leader's particular situation. It utilizes over 25 tools to help leaders reflect, assess, envision, plan, discuss and execute on what will make them — and their teams — successful. *The Ascending Leader* introduces 10 key tools and effectively explains their best situational application. Diane and Karen have artfully identified the barriers to leader success and then skillfully crafted this road map to success.

It's working for us. At this publishing, over 125 leaders at multiple levels have either completed or are currently participating in the Program. And nearly all have been retained and are performing at a high level. This retention and productivity translates to millions of dollars. As we have reviewed the program with other leaders, a common response is, "I wish we would have had this in place when I took on my role." A key component of our program is LEI Consulting's certification of our Assimilation Coaches. These coaches have mastered the tools and are providing tremendous support to our transitioning leaders.

Our Leader Assimilation Program has been a huge win for the company. We know if we catch our leaders early in their new roles and help them achieve early success, we can transform a potentially rocky road into a paved freeway. Fortunately, through targeted coaching and mentoring, we were able to help Mitch turn his performance around. When he takes on his next role, he will get all the support he needs to transition effectively, engage his team and achieve business objectives.

Thanks to the principles and tools provided in *The Ascending Leader*, we are enabling our leaders to accelerate their transitions and to thrive in their new roles.

Brent Carter
Vice President, Leader Assimilation Program Manager
Fifth Third Bank

Introduction

Congratulations! You are finally transitioning into the new role you have eagerly anticipated. You have a seat at the table and the future looks bright. What's your game plan for the next 90 days? 6 months? Do you know the team you'll be working with? Do you have a firm grasp on the organization and culture? How familiar are you with your new manager? These issues, if not thought through, can quickly overwhelm even the best-trained leaders.

Every day, people across the globe are promoted into exciting new roles. A VP of Operations is offered the COO role, starting the following week ... a Finance Director takes a VP of Finance role for a new company ... A Manager of Nursing is asked to lead a division as the Nursing Director. Sadly, at least one of these three leaders is at risk for failure according to the data and our coaching experience.

4 of 10 promoted leaders fail in the first 18 months!

More than 75% of the reason for failure is poor assimilation, according to various studies by *Harvard Business Review*, the Center for Creative Leadership and Manchester Partners International.

The costs of these failures are immeasurable, in both human and economic terms. The fallout includes everything from missed milestones to disgruntled employees, peeved peers and the exodus of talented people, not to mention the leaders' own misery. Surely it is in the interest of everyone involved for these leaders to succeed.

> **More than 75% of the reason for failure is poor assimilation**

Despite the failure rate and its toll, leaders are typically expected to make important career transitions with little or no support. Naturally, this causes a significant amount of anxiety and, left unmanaged, can cause you to derail. Stress escalates as you are expected to contribute immediately while building credibility in all relationships. A complex challenge to say the least!

While there are multiple reasons why you could derail, a few primary contributors to consider include:

- Limited awareness and management of stress behaviors may alienate others or cause you to be overcome by the chaos and crisis of the day.
- Lack of a working understanding of the organization and its culture can lead to poor structure and talent decisions, or missed culture cues.
- Relationship missteps can lead to low perceived adaptability and credibility as a leader.
- Lack of, or poorly articulated, vision and plan can have unintended consequences, such as lack of clear direction and uninspiring leadership.

A new role is stressful! And you can proactively manage the transition to significantly reduce the risk of failure. It is imperative to understand:

Why do so many promoted leaders fail in new roles?

How can you make sure the odds aren't stacked against you?

We have dedicated the past sixteen years to helping leaders like you gain the self-awareness and insight to lead while under tremendous stress in times of transition. Along the way, we have coached leaders to overcome the Enemies of a successful transition and to thrive in their new role. Importantly, the process herein will prepare you to gain credibility as a leader, aggregate knowledge to articulate a compelling vision, and develop a focused business plan that will be executed by an engaged team.

So, to begin with the end in mind, the process illustrated at the top of the next page provides an overview of this journey. It is tied to the specific strategies and tools listed on page 14 (and described throughout this book) to help you conquer the seven Enemies of your success.

7 — Develop an aligned vision and business plan to achieve results

6 — Invest to engage and inspire your team

5 — Create strong relationships with stakeholders and peers

4 — Calibrate with your manager to meet expectations

3 — Gain the organization and culture knowledge to navigate successfully

2 — Learn enough to understand the business you are expected to lead

1 — Leverage self-awareness to be seen as a credible leader in the new role

A successful transition requires a vision, a plan and the belief that your time investment up front will yield very high returns while mitigating the risk of failure.

The Enemies featured in this book are the obstacles that leaders typically face. When neglected or overlooked, they can take you down; therefore, they must be addressed for success.

Navigation of these Enemies greatly increases your probability to thrive in a new role. In this book, we challenge leaders to accurately assess their own vulnerabilities, behaviors and tendencies under stress, and to create and execute plans that will cultivate strong relationships and results. Once a leader understands him/herself and how he/she is perceived by others, it is easier to adapt to a new role and organization, as well as make the necessary adjustments to transition effectively. Optimal transitioning is particularly challenging because the process and expectations to succeed in the new role are often unclear and support is often limited at best. This book offers a comprehensive approach with proven strategies to overcome the Enemies, along with tools to support an effective transition.

Enemy to Overcome	Transition Strategy	Tool(s)
1. Submit to the Enemy Within	Conquer the Enemy Within	Personal Leader Assessment
2. Yield to the Chaos	Manage the Chaos	Leader Success Inventory
3. Misread Culture Cues	Master Culture Cues	Quick Culture Assessment
4. Misfire with Your Manager	Calibrate With Your Manager	Manager Discussion Guide
5. Overlook Stakeholders and Peers	Connect with Stakeholders and Peers	5a. Stakeholder Assessment and Strategy Plan 5b. Peer Discussion Guide
6. Alienate Your Team	Engage With Your Team	6a. Team Member Discussion Guide 6b. Team Assimilation Meeting Guide
7. Sub-Optimize Your Vision and Plan	Inspire With Your Vision and Business Plan	7a. Aligned Vision Worksheet 7b. Business Plan

What this book is not: This book is not about recruitment and pre-hire needs for new leaders — other authors have captured those areas, as well as key situations a new leader may face, very nicely in the books we've noted. We begin once a leader has been hired or promoted into their new role. The transition strategies presented in each chapter are in sequence, as are the process and tools to guide your success. Naturally, though, this is also a *flexible process* and any tool that adds value to your transition may be used at any time.

Something to note before moving on: given the importance of the new leadership role in your career, if you have the opportunity to enlist the assistance of a trusted internal or external coach as a guide and sounding board, we highly encourage it. The process and tools of this book can provide the structure, and a talented coach can help bring richness and depth to the experience.

Besides coaching leaders ourselves, we have partnered with internal Human Resources organizations to develop and certify internal HR coaches, building internal capability and ensuring the assimilation program becomes self-sustaining.

We are passionate about developing leaders and hope this book opens new doors for you to achieve your aspirations now and in each future role.

A Fable:

Got the Job!

"Annie! Annie! I got it! I got the promotion!"

Pete Colbin bounded up the steps of his house and threw open the front door with all the triumphant flourish of Caesar entering Rome. Medium height and lean with dark brown hair, Pete stood excitedly in the doorway as he heard his wife's happy squeal from an upstairs bedroom.

"Oh, Pete," cried Annie as she flew down the steps. *"Divisional Vice President! What did they say? Have you seen your new office? How much is the increase?"*

Questions poured out of Annie's laughing lips as she grilled him and hugged him at the same time. Pete laughed, pleased that she too was so excited. He knew the extra money would make it far easier to help pay off her medical school loans, which had been dragging behind them like a black anchor for several years now.

"It's not just the money, Pete, though God knows this house needs a ton of work," Annie said.

Pete knew where she was heading and began to grin.

"You," she poked her index finger into his chest, *"Are on your way up, young man,"* Annie teased.

"Thirty-seven and already a Vice President. How does that make you feel?"

"Why Ma'am," he playfully drawled in a politician's bass voice, *"it makes me mighty proud. Mighty proud, indeed."* shaking his jowls from side to side.

Annie smiled, then took a serious tone and said, *"No, really Pete. How does it make you feel?"*

"In truth? Proud but nervous; confident, but I have some reservations. Hey, I know I deserve it but I don't know if the people I'll be managing will think so. Or my new peers."

"That sounds scary," said Annie.

"I know I'm a pretty smart guy, but part of me thinks everyone will think I'm smarter than I actually am, especially now. Am I expected to know more than I did yesterday because I have a new title today?"

"It's funny," said Annie. *"You work so hard for a promotion, thinking, 'If I can only get this, everything will be better.' And when it finally comes, when you finally get it, you find, yeah, it's better but there are still problems and challenges to face, just different ones."*

They sat quietly for a moment, gazing out the picture window. Across their backyard they saw the new neighbor fixing the light over his back door.

"Have you met the new neighbors yet?" Pete asked.

"Just the husband," replied Annie. *"His name is Max something-or-other. I don't remember their last name. James or Jansen... something like that. He seemed nice. He just retired. We didn't talk that long."*

Pete and Annie returned to the exciting new topic at hand, talking about all the things the new promotion would mean for them. They finally went to bed around 11:00 PM, totally unsuspecting the role Max Something-or-other would play in their lives over the next few months.

****

~ **Chapter 1** ~

Getting Started

The next morning, nervous and excited about going to work with his new title and in a different division, Pete opened his car door and threw in his briefcase. The noise of footsteps and heavy breathing caused him to glance to his right where he spotted his new neighbor, Max, carrying a couple of large cardboard boxes from his garage to his house, obviously straining in the process.

"You're Max, right?" He called. *"I'm Pete Colbin. Let me give you a hand with that."*

Smiling and puffing as he transferred the boxes into Pete's arms, the older man said, *"Yes, I'm Max. And thanks so much, Pete. You're a life saver."* He scooted ahead and opened the front door for Pete, then followed him inside.

"Just put them down anywhere. I'll empty them during the day," said Max. *"Hey, I saw you running into the house last evening. You looked pretty excited. Everything OK?"*

Pete studied Max for a moment, taking in his grey hair and blue eyes. He looked between 65 and 70 years old, and seemed unassuming and friendly. There was a quiet self-confidence about him in the way he stood and talked.

Pete, considering all this, wondered how much he should share. The honest interest and concern in Max's eyes put Pete at ease, so, he told Max about the new promotion and, surprising himself, also about his concerns related to his new position as well.

When Pete finished, Max smiled and asked, *"Do you feel you've earned this shot at leadership?"*

"Absolutely," Pete said. *"I've done all that was expected of me and more on my way to this job."*

"But..." Max prodded.

"But people will look at me differently now, thinking I'm something special and somehow changed, that now I have all the answers. Well, I know I don't and I hate the idea of people thinking I was the wrong choice."

Max nodded and said, *"Don't want to be just another Pete from the Peter Principle, eh?"*

"Exactly," Pete said and laughed.

Max pointed to the two big boxes they had just carried in. *"See those?"* He asked. *"Those are what my wife and I call my 'Memory Vault.' Memorabilia of things I've done in my life — things I've done well and some not so well. But each item has a special meaning for me."*

Pete asked, *"Why would you save mementos of things you didn't do well?"*

"Most people don't learn that much from the victories in their lives. Oh, they celebrate success, but they rarely

think about how they did it; but the bad things, the failures — that's another story."

Max sat down on one of the boxes. *"Once, early on in my career,"* he began, *"I took over a new role in the company, managing new people, an impressive new title, same as you. Well, I started shooting out memos, orders and directions right away to show how smart and aggressive I was. Then I wondered why people weren't responding well to me as a leader."* He smiled and shook his head ruefully.

"And?" Pete asked, now clearly interested.

"And," Max replied, *"several of those misguided memos are still in that box and they've saved me from repeating those mistakes later on. There have been a lot of times in my career when I've needed to touch base with who I've been and how I've behaved."*

Max pointed to the boxes. *"I'd go to the 'vault', revisit the good and wallow around in the bad for a while and then manage myself toward how I wanted to be going forward."*

"Kind of a self-analysis," Pete said.

"Exactly. I'd go there to reflect on the person in the box...the smart and the not-so smart. Everything from Little League trophies and business award plaques, to those terrible memos and other flubbed opportunities."

Pete said, *"I really feel that I've earned my way to this point, but I know I've still got a ton to learn. I just don't want to blow it."*

"*Try to push negative impulses like that from your mind.*" Max offered. "*Go into your own 'Memory Vault' and revisit who you are and remember all the things you accomplished to win this promotion. Fight the urge to be an instant leader. Be patient and use the skills that got you here to help you learn and adapt to the new role.*"

Pete listened thoughtfully and thanked Max for his interest, wondering where this guy got his information. It made sense but seemed a little simplistic. Still, Max gave him some good confidence-building thoughts to keep in mind going into his first day.

****

~~Submit to~~ **Conquer the Enemy Within**

Key Questions:

- What kinds of stress behaviors do you need to be aware of and manage?

- What impact did they have? How did you manage them?

- What can you do differently now to identify and manage stress behaviors in this role?

Starting in a new role after earning that sought-after promotion is an exciting time, full of promise and opportunity. Thinking of the positive impact you can have and the results you and your team will achieve can be exhilarating ... and, if you are like most transitioning leaders, especially in today's warp-speed workplace, you may soon feel overwhelmed and under pressure to perform. The stress associated with the transition makes it tempting to submit to the enemy within. This is the first challenge to overcome as a transitioning leader. The voice inside your head can fill a new leader's thoughts with the sense of overwhelm, the fear of failure, and/or the need to prove your value too quickly, which drives your behavior and how you are perceived by others.

Impact to You: If you give in to your stress behaviors, you may inadvertently turn people off or have people feel disconnected to you as a leader! This stress behavior seldom inspires others to follow.

Career transitions are stressful no matter how well planned:

- A new location, new boss, new team, new key stakeholders, new peers, new goals, and new expectations — it can be stressful just thinking about it all!
- In a new role we are wrestling with vulnerability, stress and change. It is important to understand that we all have different coping styles under stress and during change.
- The new role often requires skills and/or capabilities that we may not have mastered yet.
- The change coupled with stress can cause a leader to submit to stress behaviors versus proactively making choices that contribute to success...we know because we've been there!
- The BIG opportunity is to conquer the enemy within by effectively managing anxiety and stress, and develop new skills to build credibility as well as resonance in your relationships.

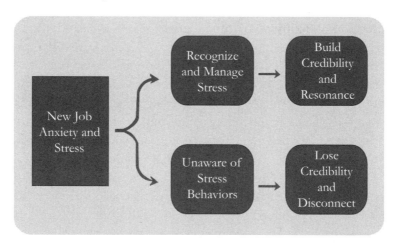

No doubt you have heard the oft-quoted phrase, *"We have met the enemy and he is us."* That quote, from Walt Kelly's Pogo comic strip of the early 1950s, captures what we know all too well — sometimes we just need to get out of our own way!

Of course, we each have our own way of dealing with anxiety; the key is to be aware of the impact of anxiety and stress, and to be honest with yourself about any areas for development or skill gaps you may need to address. With awareness you can choose to gain greater self-awareness and use that understanding to manage behaviors and actions in ways that are more positive and productive.

> *"As a highly sought after thought partner, trusted advisor and facilitator of leaders' learning, I partner with leaders consumed by both the accelerating velocity of change and uncertainty in a new role.* The Ascending Leader *can be that much needed Game-Changer.* The Ascending Leader *heightens leaders' awareness and desire to pause, reflect and respect the uniqueness and complexity of each new environment and equips them with both the tools and the road map to purposefully and intentionally actualize their desired vision."*
>
> — Bonnie Newland, PhD,
> Director of Coaching for Fifth Third Bank

Do any of the following stress behaviors look familiar? If so, it will be helpful to be aware of your own tendencies in order to manage and avoid submitting to the enemy within, as follows:

Isolating yourself: Though this is very tempting because you feel vulnerable and want to be seen as competent, this is not the time to go it alone! Please, reach out and ask for the help you need; it is a great way to build relationships, learn and help overcome your sense of isolation. Take advantage of being-new-to-the-role as an opportunity to ask questions and more questions....

Knowing it all: Coming off as a know-it-all or referring often to success in a past role or company is a big turn-off! Trust that you will be valued and give yourself the gift of time to prove what you can do in the present. Resist the temptation to impart all of your wisdom or compare past successes to the current situation.

Focusing on the wrong things: Spending time and energy where you are most comfortable versus where the need exists in the business, is easy to do under stress! Seek feedback in the new role to validate the needs of the business and be sure your time, attention and actions reflect your desire to fully understand the highest priority business needs and to address them.

Being too aggressive: Thinking that the way to win is to immediately take charge won't work! It is your willingness to show vulnerability in order to learn and understand something new that is the true test of leadership.

Needing to be liked: Building relationships that are available versus strategic is highly inefficient and can limit credibility. Purposefully seek connections that are based on mutual respect, shared vision and values. This will inevitably help you build productive, strategic relationships.

Appearing to be out for yourself: Seeking information and knowledge that is to your benefit alone is risky business. Be collaborative versus competitive and you will achieves success!

Repeating old habits: Thinking the way to be successful in a new role is just like the previous role can cause a poor start. Instead, adapt to the new environment by understanding the unique organization, culture, political environment, leaders and how to achieve results in the new role. For example, leaders who struggle to delegate will find similar challenges in a new role.

Neglecting your own well-being: Getting so focused on work that you neglect essentials like sleep, good nutrition, exercise, spending time with loved ones and friends, or your spiritual needs can lead you down a very unhealthy path. Don't underestimate the detrimental impact this can have; keep an eye on these things and proactively manage them so you can function at your highest level.

Leveraging Matthew Kelly's concept of people becoming "the best version of themselves," it is possible to deeply resonate with others as a transitioning leader by conquering the enemy within and being the very best version of you. Kelly is a well-known author and motivational speaker who has dedicated his life to helping people achieve their *"best version."* In his latest book, *Off Balance,* he shares a system for achieving long-term professional and personal satisfaction. It is a great resource for any leader — especially one in transition.

Client's Story: Renee

In October 2011, Renee was hired to lead the Commercial line of business for one of her new organization's 16 markets. She had quite a glowing track record as well as a high performing team at her former company, where she had spent the prior 16 years. When discussing expectations and outcomes with her new manager, the market president, it was apparent that Renee had her work cut out for her. She had to engage her team under new leadership, learn the market, connect with clients, build relationships with corporate executives, gain insights from her peers, establish a strategic plan ... oh, and grow the business by 160%.

True to her nature, Renee jumped in with both feet, learning as much as she could by attending meetings, gaining input from her team and asking a lot of questions. As is typical, her team was used to the former leader's approach and style. She had to work hard to gain their trust and engage them in new ways of doing things. While she listened to their ideas, Renee was also convinced that some things needed to be different. She strived to respect the culture and the experience of her team, yet invoke changes that she believed would be best for the organization and grow the business. The challenges of invoking change, gaining the commitment of her team, securing advocacy from her president and other senior leaders and dealing with the stressors of high expectations all converged in a perfect storm that shook her confidence.

Fortunately for Renee, she had support. She took advantage of the company's new leader assimilation program, and she had a coach, Diana, with whom to confide and seek counsel. Among other things, she quickly recognized that, despite her prior success, she needed to prove herself in a new company. Over the course of the next several months, Renee was able to work through the challenges, build key relationships and get on solid footing with her team. There were many contributors to her ability to turn the situation around. Importantly, she allowed herself to open up with her coach about her doubts and challenges, and identified strategies for moving forward.

With her coach's guidance, Renee took advantage of some key tools from the leader assimilation program and took the necessary steps to achieve success. The Leader Success Inventory helped her crystallize her priorities and separate her emotions from what needed to be done. She formed an internal advisory group and leveraged the helpful advice of peers in other regions. She identified and consistently maintained a meeting operating rhythm with direct reports as well as the broader team. She also facilitated team assimilation meetings and team building activities. She stayed in touch with her president and kept her actions focused and purposeful.

In addition to the leader assimilation program, Renee benefitted greatly from attending The Leadership Challenge®, a core leadership course for senior leaders that not only immersed participants in important leadership tenets, but also provided the opportunity for 360 degree feedback. She took the feedback to heart and re-centered on the capabilities and experience she brought to the table. With renewed confidence and vigor, she accepted her own leadership challenge and set out to rally her team around a new vision.

Renee's team became one of the top performing commercial markets in the company in 2012! Looking back on her experience, Renee realizes that her biggest challenge was herself, allowing self-doubt to temporarily overshadow her instincts and better judgment. She now looks to the future with optimism and enthusiasm.

****

In his bestselling book, *What Got You Here Won't Get You There,* Marshall Goldsmith outlines 20 "transactional flaws performed by one person against others." The behaviors outlined provide keen insights for those who are courageous enough to do an honest self-assessment and earnestly strive to control these flaws. This book is an excellent source of information for further reading to seek greater self- awareness and ultimately self- management of behaviors that can derail a leader.

Besides the resources we've noted above, there are countless other ways to build your self-awareness, a critical foundation for success in a leadership role. Many find journaling to be a valuable approach. Self assessment instruments like the Myers-Briggs Type Indicator, Strengths Based Leadership, DISC, and other such tools can be quite helpful, particularly with the aid of a talented coach or facilitator.

Another key way is to ask for honest feedback from someone with whom you have built a trusting relationship. Ask about strengths as well as areas for improvement. As a colleague once said: "Listen as if they are right!" This also holds for listening to helpful developmental advice from your manager. You can always review the feedback and determine its validity, but if you get defensive and never really hear it in the first place, you won't have the opportunity to benefit from it.

> "Talent is God-given.
> Be humble.
>
> Fame is man-given.
> Be grateful.
>
> Conceit is self-given.
> Be careful."
>
> — John Wooden

Tool #1: Personal Leader Assessment

What is it?

A guide to help you identify behaviors and potential skill/capability gaps that could contribute to your derailment. Once recognized, strategies can be identified to overcome them to build credibility as well as more resonance in relationships.

Why use it?

It is helpful to honestly self-assess strengths to leverage, areas for development as well as potential skill gaps. Dedicated self-reflection can help you manage the potential issues early and help you to avoid the inadvertent behavioral mistakes and/or missteps that so many leaders make.

How to make the most of it?

1. Review the tool, keeping all of your experience up to this point in mind, as well as the demands and skills required of the now role.

   o Note your key strengths, areas for development and skills needed for the new role.

2. Assess how you have behaved during transitions into new leadership roles in the past. Rate yourself on the outlined stress behaviors and reflect on key insights.

   o The *"Your Insights"* section is a guide for reflection on your past transitions into new roles, to understand strengths that can be leveraged and areas for concern to be managed.

   o Identify possible strategies to take advantage of.

3. The blank section at the bottom is as valuable as the rest of this tool — each of us has unique stress behaviors; if we take the time to consider them and bring them out into

the open, we have a fighting chance at managing them. Left hidden, they will continue to haunt us.

4. It can be quite helpful to discuss this with a trusted colleague, friend and/or significant other, not to mention your coach, if you have one.

Personal Leader Assessment

Based on past experience and the demands of the new role, what are the strengths you will need for success in the new role? What areas will need development?

Strengths (Skills/Capabilities and Behaviors):	Areas for Development (Skills/Capabilities and Behaviors):
Patience

Relationship building

Willingness to learn

• Relationship Building
• Team Development
• Creativity | Technical knowledge

Patience

• Commitment to learning

• Following through |

Instructions:

Read the stress behaviors and indicate on a scale of 1 to 5, where 1 is *"not at all"* and 5 is *"all of the time"*, whether the stress behavior is of concern. Make notes in the Your Insights section to ensure your success!

get roster manageable this week so I can spend more time with Brittany next three weeks

Identify Potential Stress Behaviors to Avoid	Impact on Others	Rating	Your Insights	Possible Strategies
Isolating yourself: though this is very tempting because you feel vulnerable and want to be seen as competent, this is not the time to go it alone.	Others will hesitate to connect with you if you are not accessible, available and proactively developing relationships.	3	"Reserved about not being a bother to Brittany" Not worried about doing this w/ direct reports	• Reach out to ask for help you need; it is a great way to build relationships, learn, and help overcome your sense of isolation. • Take advantage of being new to the role as an opportunity to ask many, many questions. • Schedule time daily to build relationships and alliances. • Allow time to develop informal relationships that enhance accessibility.
Knowing it all: coming off as a know-it-all or referring often to success in a past role or company is a big turn-off!	Others may discount your contributions, assume you are arrogant or that you lack confidence and/or are unwilling to adapt.	4	don't feel like I have resources Team members know more than me	• Trust that you will be valued and give yourself the gift of time to earn credibility. • Resist comparing past successes to the current situation. • Ask lots of clarifying questions and share insights to check for understanding. • Acknowledge previous successes and contributions of others.

Identify Potential Stress Behaviors to Avoid	Impact on Others	Rating	Your Insights	Possible Strategies
Focusing on the wrong things: spending time and energy where you are most comfortable, versus where the need is in the business, is easy to do under stress.	Seen as marginally effective and lacking in enterprise view of the business.	4	Comfort zone is largely consumed what are our highest priorities	• Seek feedback to validate the needs of the business and be sure your time, attention and actions reflect your understanding of the highest priorities. • Define focus with your Manager and seek feedback consistently on highest priorities in the first six months.
Being too aggressive: thinking that the way to win is to immediately take charge seldom works.	Seen as impulsive, lacking in emotional intelligence and business acumen.	1	More enthusiastic than aggressive	• Show vulnerability by learning and understanding something new. • Resist making significant changes until all key stakeholders, Manager and team have provided input to your priorities.
Needing to be liked: building relationships that are available versus strategic is highly inefficient and can be a can be a liability to your credibility.	Seen as a marginal performer if not building strategic relationships. Can be viewed as an operational versus strategic leader.	2	Pertains to direct reports lower if for external partners	• Purposefully seek connections based on mutual respect, shared vision and values. This inevitably helps you build productive, strategic relationships. • Seek to build relationships and be respected by sharing insights about vision, mission and values. Other thought leaders will become engaged.

Identify Potential Stress Behaviors to Avoid	Impact on Others	Rating	Your Insights	Possible Strategies
Appearing to be out for yourself: seeking information and knowledge that is to your benefit alone is risky business!	Seen as self-centered and self-involved versus interested in what is best for others.	1		• Foster collaboration, not competition, and you will achieve success in a new role. • Actively seek information about serving the interests of others and incorporate what is best for others into priorities and communication.
Repeating old habits: thinking the way to be successful in a new role is just like the previous role can get you off to a poor start.	Not adapting to the new organization and culture can cause missteps and a failure to connect with other leaders.	3	*I think I can do this but my role is so different I can't lean on past*	• Adapt to the new environment by understanding the unique organization, culture, political environment, people and how to achieve results in the new role. • Be very observant. Check for understanding of the culture, how work is accomplished and who should be influenced to succeed in the role.

Neglecting well-being: overlooking essentials like sleep, good nutrition, exercise, spending time with loved ones and friends, or your spiritual needs.	Over time, a toll is taken on you, your family and those you work with.	3	*Love my leisure time, but don't want to work (exercise) outside office*	• Recognize that you are not super-human!
				• Conduct a well-being check and make adjustments:
				  o In what aspects are you taking good care of yourself?
				  o What areas are not getting enough attention?
				  o What areas are you ignoring altogether?!

Other Stress Behaviors to be Aware of and Manage:				

~Chapter Summary~

Know Thyself!

Transitioning to a new role creates stress. Addressing stress behaviors and knowledge/ skill gaps are essential components of your success.

Like so many things in life, we can be our own worst enemy, or we can step up, own the knowledge, skill or behavioral challenges we may not like to admit, and take action. It is the courageous leader who takes a good hard look in the mirror and makes adjustments.

Now, starting from a base of improved self-awareness and a strategy to combat the negative voices that creep into your head, it's time to take a look at the next enemy of success: the chaos that comes with transition, managing the new duties, new expectations, new people, new processes, etc.

~ Chapter 2 ~

Feeling Overwhelmed

Several days later, Pete pulled into his driveway and caught sight of Max hoeing the flower beds along the side of his new home. Exiting the car, he waved to Max and said, *"Thanks again for your advice. It came in handy."* While his statement was made out of courtesy, Pete was surprised to think, *"You know, it really did. Simple as it was, it was just what I needed to keep in mind."*

"My pleasure, Pete. I hope it's going well for you," Max replied.

Pete walked over to where Max was digging and the two men chatted for a few minutes about the virtues of hoeing versus roto-tilling. It was an easy back-and-forth conversation that eventually turned to Pete's new promotion. Pete confided that while work was going pretty well, he was feeling a bit overwhelmed. He drew a steep line in the air with the flat of his hand.

"The learning curve feels almost vertical. There's so much new coming at me, sometimes I feel like I'm barely keeping afloat."

Max asked a couple of questions and Pete gave a few examples. It was obvious to Pete that Max was pulling these questions from some past business experience.

Finally, Max said, *"You know, Pete, a similar thing happened to me when I moved into the role of General Manager at a commercial bank some years ago."*

Pete nodded but said nothing. *"General Manager?"* He thought to himself, *"Pretty good job, I'd say."*

"I remember the steep learning curve and the chaos going on as I was trying to learn. Kind of like the weeds in this garden. I had to learn what's a weed and what's a plant and then get rid of the weeds." He smiled, *"While trying not to kill my wife's expensive plants. It's a lot more difficult in a new job of course. I'm not trying to play it down."*

Before he could stop himself, Pete asked, *"What did you do?"* He quickly added, *"If you don't mind my asking?"*

"I'm afraid it's pretty basic stuff, Pete. I just started to think of that chaos as my enemy. And you don't give in to your enemies, do you? So you just can't give in to the chaos of the new job. Your challenge is to make sense of it and you can't do that unless you understand it."

Max frowned a bit, remembering. *"I forced myself to learn more about that job and all the things it entailed better than anyone had done before me. My mantra was: 'You can't truly manage what you don't understand.' So I made time for learning; early mornings, late nights, whenever I could fit it in."*

Pete thanked Max for his time and advice and excused himself for dinner. On his way back to the house he thought, *"Who is this guy and where does he get this stuff? Weeds and mantras?"*

Max's words stayed with Pete all evening and on his way to work the next day:

*"You can't truly manage
what you don't understand."*

****

*You can't truly manage
what you dont understand*

Key Questions:

- How can you get up to speed about the business while managing the multitude of day-to-day demands (and not getting swallowed up by them)?

- What have you done to organize and prioritize your learning so you can be most effective in your new role?

With so many demands and so little time, is it any wonder that transitioning to a new role feels chaotic?! Yielding to the Chaos occurs when a leader does not allow the time to learn comprehensively about the business and its complexities, and instead becomes consumed by the crisis of the day — day after day. Rather than assessing the needs of the business and allowing essential time for learning before leading, the leader becomes mired in the minutia.

Impact to You: First impressions count! If you can't conquer this enemy, you may be seen as an operational versus strategic leader and miss the opportunity to develop key relationships that are vital to your success. You may lose opportunities to build credibility in order to contribute more strategically.

Leaders who see the big picture and have strategic insight also have the greatest propensity for success! They understand that in order to fully perform, they need to gain a broad view by learning about the organization, culture, strategic relationships, manager and team. With this accelerated learning a leader can quickly aggregate knowledge, create an aligned vision and plan to prioritize, focus and achieve results.

> "It's a lack of clarity that creates chaos and frustration. These emotions are poison to any living goal."
>
> — Steve Maraboli

Strategies That Work:

1. Understand that a comprehensive approach (such as the Leader Success Inventory below) will work to quickly build your credibility. Observe and listen in all settings to maximize learning first, then contribute with higher competence.
2. Request your Manager's undivided attention to help you gain critical knowledge, swiftly, and seek his/her support for your learning before you are expected to fully contribute.
3. Identify and develop strategic relationships in all aspects of your role and responsibilities.
4. Use all available resources wisely — consider HR, Finance, functional leaders, team members and peers to gain knowledge quickly.

The Leader Success Inventory (LS Inventory) outlined below is your guide to organize and prioritize learning, avoid becoming overwhelmed, and ultimately arrive at an aligned vision and business plan that will lead to success.

The Ascending Leader

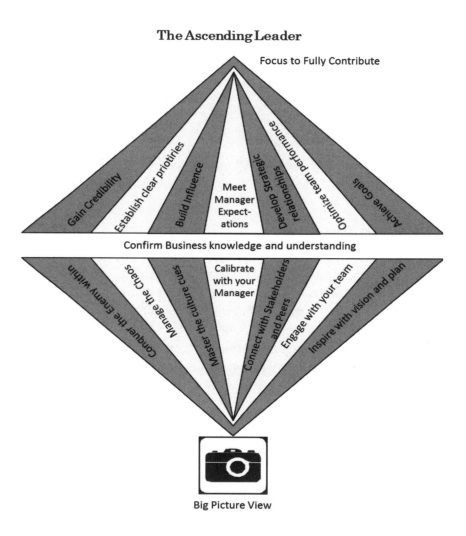

Focus to Fully Contribute

Gain Credibility

Establish clear priotiries

Build Influence

Meet Manager Expect- ations

Develop Strategic relationships

Optimize team performance

Achieve Goals

Confirm Business knowledge and understanding

Conquer the Enemy within

Manage the Chaos

Master the culture cues

Calibrate with your Manager

Connect with Stakeholders and Peers

Engage with your team

Inspire with vision and plan

Big Picture View

Client's Story: Brad

Brad, a newly promoted CFO located in Atlanta, was working through his transition with the support of Susan, the Human Resources Director. Brad was highly intelligent and incredibly talented; however, he had so much more to learn and understand about the culture and individuals he was now leading. While Brad was familiar with the organization since he had worked there for many years, the CFO responsibilities and his Sr. Executive peers were all new to him. To confirm his business knowledge and gauge his understanding of the areas he would need to focus on, Brad completed the Leader Success Inventory.

Once he completed the LS Inventory, Brad shared this information with his direct Manager and they discussed and agreed upon Brad's knowledge & prioritization ratings. As a result, Brad and his Manager were able to quickly identify two key areas of strength that Brad would need to leverage in his new role and two specific areas of focus for Brad's development in the coming months.

Two key high priority strengths for Brad from the LS Inventory included #1 and #2 in the "Sponsorship Relationships" section: 1.) "I understand who the key strategic leaders in the organization are who have influence over my business," and, 2.) "I have identified sponsors who are essential to the achievement of my goals and have begun to build relationships, discuss roles, and define desired outcomes with them." It was also very evident that there were two key areas of development that Brad needed to focus on to be successful. Those two areas were #1 and #2 in the "My Team" section of the tool: 1.) "I have inspired the team with my vision, seeking their input and gaining momentum to achieve results" and, 2.) "I have defined a communication plan and feedback processes with input from the team."

In the weeks to follow, Brad focused on leveraging the relationships he had built with influential leaders, peers, and sponsors to create an aligned vision and strategic communication plan that established his credibility and

45

aligned his organization toward a common goal. This simple but profound exercise built a clear foundation of knowledge and understanding for Brad, and acted as a springboard from which he effectively built a strategic plan for the first 90 days that took his influence & organizational competence to a new level.

For Brad, the LS Inventory provided him with clarity of direction and allowed him to focus his energies and efforts toward activities that created real progress toward achieving his individual, team, and organizational goals. By utilizing the LS Inventory, Brad was able to "manage the chaos" of his transition into his new role and lead his organization to great success — a success that they still enjoy to this day.

Tool #2: Leader Success Inventory (LS Inventory)

Whatever your circumstances — newly promoted, transitioning to a new role and/or new to the organization —the LS Inventory will help you learn all you need to know to fully contribute faster!

What is it?

A comprehensive tool to help you consider all elements associated with success in the role, including:

- *Leadership Role*: Gain insights about adapting professionally and personally.
- *Organization/Culture*: Build knowledge and understanding to navigate successfully in the role.
- *Manager Relationship*: Clarify expectations between you and your Manager.
- *Peer and Stakeholder Relationships*: Capture learning and build the foundation of productive, strategic relationships.
- *Team Assimilation*: Inspire and develop credibility with your team.
- *Business Plan*: Create a comprehensive plan to ensure results.

When to use it?

In the first 30 days!

Why use it?

To assess current knowledge, seek input from others and identify priorities in order to create an Action Plan for a successful transition into the role. To be clear, this is not a business plan, it is a tool to capture the knowledge, support and actions needed to create a successful business plan in the 90–120 day time frame.

How to make the most of it?

1. Review and rate your knowledge of the LS Inventory elements and note action items.
   o Be honest in your self-assessment; the point is to leverage strengths and to identify gaps to fill.
2. Discuss the LS Inventory with your Manager — seek answers, input, support and advice.
3. Know you can't do it all at once, so identify priorities and action items by area.
4. Establish immediate priorities.
   o At the end of the LS Inventory, capture immediate priorities for the business with the help of your Manager (the everyday needs that require immediate attention).
5. As you take action, solicit help from others, including your team, peers and other stakeholders.
   o Typically people enjoy sharing their knowledge, experience and suggestions to help others succeed. At the same time, you will be building vital relationships and your professional network through the process.

Leader Success Inventory

Please read the statements in each section and rate your knowledge on a scale of 1 to 5, with (1) unfamiliar to (5) comprehensive knowledge. Also, indicate 1, 2, or 3 as highest priority areas to pursue learning in the priority column. Indicate action items to accelerate learning toward full contribution.

My Leadership Role	Rating	Priority	Action Items
1. I understand the strategic and operational imperatives for the business and my area of responsibility.	3		
2. I possess the technical knowledge, leadership capabilities and cultural understanding that will be required of me in this new role.	3	1	
3. I have developed a personal vision for success in this role and seek feedback to compare with my own perceptions.	2		
4. I have developed an aligned vision for the future of the business that includes other leaders' input.	1		
5. I have been able to effectively balance the workload in my new role with responsibilities at home.	5		
6. If I experience work and life stress, I am comfortable seeking assistance to support my individual and family needs.	5		

Organization/Culture	Rating	Priority	Action Items
1. I understand the organization's vision, purpose and value proposition; their alignment in my areas of responsibility is apparent.	3		
2, Adequate infrastructure, technology and processes are in place to support our strategies.	2		
3. When executing, the organization follows standardized processes rather than relying on individual execution.			
4. I have developed a plan for building relationships with key customers and internal stakeholders (see Sponsor Relationships below).			
5. I understand how financial targets are established and how associated strategies and goals are aligned.			
6. I understand how key decisions are made and who needs to be involved.			
7. I understand and can navigate the organization's structure.			
8. We have processes to recognize and acknowledge outstanding performance.			
9. Formal and informal communication processes are clear and barriers to effective communication are removed.			
10. The work culture is positive; inclusions, engagement and development are encouraged and supported.			

My Manager	Rating	Priority	Action Items
1. My Manager and I understand how to work best with each other, regarding communication, decision making and issue escalation.	3		
2. I have discussed the priorities for the business with my Manager as a starting point for my own learning.	4		
3. I understand my Manager's expectations for results during the first year.	3		
4. I have reached agreement for an update process to keep my Manager informed of my progress in the first year.	4		
5. I understand the resources available to support my success in this new role.	4		
6. I feel comfortable approaching my Manager with new ideas, issues, challenges and support requests.	5		

Sponsor Relationships	Rating	Priority	Action Items
1. I understand who the key strategic leaders in the organization are who have influence over my business.			
2. I have identified sponsors essential to the achievement of my goals and have begun to build relationships, discuss roles and define desired outcomes with them.			
3. I have identified strategic advocates in the organization and have begun to seek their guidance and to share my vision for the business.			
4. I have developed peer relationships that have potential to become trusted advisors and sponsors.			
5. I have begun to engage key sponsors in my success as a leader in this role.			

My Team	Rating	Priority	Action Items
1. I have inspired the team with my vision, seeking their input and gaining momentum to achieve results.			
2. I have defined a communication plan and feedback processes with input from the team.			
3. There is a high degree of trust and interdependence on my team.	4		
4. I have met with my team and established expectations and a foundation for trusting work relationships.	4		
5. I have assessed the talent of the team relative to their roles and capability to achieve business results, and have the right team in place.			
6. I have created operating rhythms for meetings and performance updates that encourages accountability, individually and as a team.	3		

Business Plan	Rating	Priority	Action Items
1. I have captured adequate learning about the culture and organization to create a six-month Business Plan.			
2. I have established relationships essential to the success of the plan.			
3. I understand the business and industry environment well enough to create a six-month plan.			
4. I have shared my vision and the Business Plan concepts with my Manager and key sponsors to seek support.			
5. I have provided opportunities for input to my vision and Business Plan prior to completing the plan.			

Immediate Priorities

-
-
-
-
-

~Chapter Summary~

Manage the Chaos!

- Make the time to complete the Leader Success Inventory — to understand the big picture — it's worth it.
- Organize and prioritize knowledge to be gained and actions to be taken.
- Seek organization and culture knowledge in all interactions.
- Use the LS Inventory as an opportunity to build relationships essential to your success.
- Confirm business knowledge and understanding using the tool.
- If you skip the Leader Success Inventory you will have to come back!

With time invested in completing the LS Inventory, you have set a course to manage the chaos of your transition. With time set aside to learn the full scope of your new responsibilities, you will avoid making mistakes common to many leaders who fail. Your 90 to 120 day plan will let you navigate a clear course through the enemies you face in this phase of the transition. Looking ahead to Chapter 3, we'll explore how leaders need to understand the corporate and division culture they are now a part of and how to adapt to it.

~Chapter 3~

Navigating the Waters

A few weeks later, Pete was lighting his barbecue, getting set to grill some chicken breasts for dinner. Hearing the sound of hammering, he looked up to see Max on the roof of his house nailing down some new shingles.

"Expecting rain, Max?" Pete cracked.

"Nah," said Max, looking down from the roof. *"Just getting to know the ins and outs of my new house and the new neighborhood. How are things with you?"*

Pete moved a couple of plump chicken breasts to the low heat and walked over to the yard below the roof where Max was working.

"It's going OK," he said. *"I took your advice and really burrowed into the nooks and crannies of my new job. It seems less overwhelming already."*

Pete was all set for a big, *"I told you so!"* Max stopped hammering, just grinned and said with obvious enthusiasm, *"Way to go, Pete."*

Feeling a growing comfort around the older man, Pete volunteered more. *"All that new learning gave me a few new ideas for improved efficiencies but I'm having a bit of trouble getting buy-in from key executives."*

"Are you sure the ideas are sound?" Max asked.

"I am," replied Pete. *"I did my research and talked to all the departments involved."*

Max quietly thought for a moment. He rubbed his chin between his thumb and index finger and said, *"Remember how I just told you I was getting to know my new house and my new neighborhood?"* Pete nodded and Max continued. *"You understand — all houses have their own quirks and problems, same with most neighborhoods nowadays. There are different levels of income, different races and different religions — each resulting in a different kind of culture, if you will."*

"Yeah, I get it," said Pete.

"Well, it's the same with a new position sometimes. Take your situation. You're in a new division, managing people you didn't really know before. Everything is new and you have to get to understand how things come together and work at your new level. Same kind of thing happened to me once when I was made Director of our global operations in Asia."

Pete's eyes got a bit wider but he said nothing; Global operations!

"Talk about doing things differently!" Max continued. *"How a company or even a division does things, how it behaves...its culture...it really impacts how you should go about getting things done."*

Then Max asked, *"How have others at your level gotten upper-management approval in the past?"*

Pete didn't know. And it struck him that fitting in, understanding how to get things done and influencing to lead change in his new position might be a lot different from what he was formerly used to.

In the silence Max fiddled with his hammer, and then confided, *"A company's culture can sink a really good idea if a manager can't navigate the waters. Hey, I can smell your chicken cooking from up here. Better go see to your dinner. "*

As he returned to the grill, Pete began to suspect that Max was more than a simple retiree puttering around the house. Global operations? Was he serious? He'd have to probe a little more into old Max's background.

****

Key Questions:

- What have you observed that will be helpful to understand and adapt to the organizational culture?

- How is it the same or different from the organizational culture you are coming from?

- What can you do to navigate the culture and gain the influence needed to help you succeed?

Whether you have been hired to build upon success or to lead change, learning about the culture is key. A leader can miss essential culture cues that impact ultimate success or failure by under-estimating the importance of understanding and adapting to the culture before trying to lead change in a significant way.

Impact to You: Do you know that, according to *Harvard Business Review*, 75% of the reason executives fail in the first 18 months in a new role is due to poor culture assimilation? This typically happens for one of two reasons:

- The leader fails to adapt to the culture norms and risks being rejected, or;

- The leader fails to understand the current cultural mindsets and its impact on performance.

In various articles, leader transition expert Michael Watkins notes that, on average, moves between units in the same company are rated to be 70% as difficult as joining a new company. The primary reason in-company promotions are relatively easier is that current employees have a better understanding of, and appreciation for, their organization's culture.

Given this, the new leader is wise to learn about and adapt to the culture prior to performing or leading change initiatives by identifying:

- Key aspects of culture that will be barriers to individual and organization success, and;
- Identified culture strengths that can be leveraged quickly to achieve results.

You have been hired to get results in a new role, whether following a successful leader or one who failed to achieve results. If you, first, adapt successfully to the current culture and, second, lead the change necessary to get results, you have a much higher probability of success. Unfortunately, while culture cues are ubiquitous, they are not all apparent and some are easy to miss. Among the culture cues that are easily missed — and most critical to understand — is mindset, which is the way of thinking that drives behavior.

An iceberg is a good analogy for understanding culture. The observable part is just a fraction of the whole. The non-observable part, the elements below the surface of the water, is far larger and harder to comprehend — this is typically where culture cues are not apparent and become easy to misread. A successful leader in a new role must seek input and ask questions to gain a working knowledge of an organization's observable and non-observable culture.

Why this is true...

Observable:
Norms: communication, traditions and visible behaviors

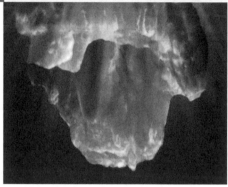

Non-Observable:
Mindset: values, beliefs and assumptions that guide behavior

"Culture eats strategy for breakfast."

—Pete Drucker

Dropping into a pre-existing culture and behaving in a way that is counter to it invites trouble. Like a foreign invader in the human body that gets rejected to keep us healthy, a perceived "enemy" in a company's culture can experience the same fate if he or she fails to adapt.

Dorothea Brande's quote, *"Old habits are strong and jealous!"* could easily be reframed with company culture in mind as *"Culture is strong and jealous!"*

In their book, *Leading Culture Change in Global Organizations*, Daniel Denison, Robert Hooijberg, Nancy Lane and Colleen Lief note, "Culture always reflects the collective wisdom that comes from the lessons people learn as they adapt and survive over time." The book is a great resource for more in-depth understanding of leading culture change in organizations. Culture assessment examples are included to demonstrate the value of accumulating knowledge about an organization's culture (using actual data gathered from employees) and leveraging results to lead culture change in an inspiring way that invites buy-in.

For transitioning leaders it is important to recognize that all organization and culture change occurs within a system. All elements of the system need to be in alignment to sustain a culture change and ultimately a new level of performance.

For instance, if a new performance management system is implemented by leadership in an organization, and managers believe it is fundamentally unfair to their teams, as well as difficult to administer, there is virtually no chance that employees will see the change as positive or the annual performance review as fair. On the other hand, if managers are given the opportunity to understand and give input to the vision for the change, and provide feedback about measurement and administration of the performance management system, the change is more likely to succeed. This way, not only is the culture change possible, but achieving the vision for improved employee performance is also possible when all elements of the system are aligned.

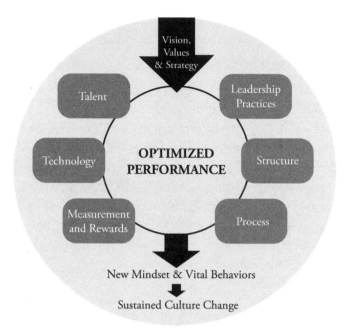

Why is it so important to understand the culture? If some elements of culture are understood and others are not, a leader may risk failure by alienating critical constituents, teams or key stakeholders in the culture. Additionally, if some elements of the system are understood and leveraged for culture change and others are not, it mitigates a leader's progress in creating and sustaining culture change. Understanding the system as the foundation for culture change and the relationships among all key stakeholders is essential to gaining cultural awareness and later influencing culture change.

So as a foundation, it is most helpful for the leader to gain an understanding of the past and present cultures in order to share and gain acceptance of a vision for the future and desired culture in the organization.

Strategies that Work:

1. Make it your goal to understand the observable and non-observable aspects of the culture in all interactions.
   - o Observable — on a continuum of "very" to "not very" please consider:
     - How formal is the work environment (furnishings, how people dress)?
     - How formal is communication among employees? Among or between leaders and employees?
     - How diverse are employees?
     - How collegial is it? Do people go to lunch together? Socialize?
     - How are employees rewarded?
     - How is conflict handled?
     - How technologically advanced is it?
     - How well is time managed? Meetings start/end on time? Deadlines set/met?
     - How formal is the climate?
   - o Non-observable:
     - How clear are the organization's vision and values? Are they articulated? Lived?
     - How are decisions made? Formal process? Hierarchical? Team-based?
     - How empowered are employees?
     - How team-oriented is it?
     - How process-oriented is it?
     - How innovative is it?
     - How well informed are employees about important aspects of the organization?
2. Be a sponge! Seek all avenues to gain greater cultural awareness: leadership practices, structure, communication, company events, conversations with colleagues, customer interactions, performance, written history of the

company, observable norms and non-observable insights that reveal cultural mindset.

- o Try to comprehend the rich context of history and experiences to understand the vision/mission of the organization.
- o Ask questions about beliefs and assumptions to uncover mindset and shared values.
- o Seek knowledge about achievement and recognition to understand what behavior is rewarded.

3. Capitalize on new learning from the Culture section on the LS Inventory, found in Chapter 2. One-on-one discussions, fueled by elements of the LS Inventory, will take you a long way.
4. Understand that it is essential to understand and adapt to the current culture and gain credibility before attempting to lead culture change. What appears familiar and not foreign is often accepted!
5. For more in-depth awareness and context, use the Culture Quick Assessment outlined below as a road map to cultural understanding based on the past, present and future.

Client's Story: Mary

Mary was transferred to the Michigan Region after several years in executive positions at the corporate headquarters. As the new President of the Western Michigan market, Mary took on the role with great expectations and little time to acclimate as an internal leader. Even though Mary was familiar with the regional structure and even some of the customers, she realized quickly she would still need to understand the history, business environment, context of the market place, the existing team, challenges, and growth opportunities.

Mary found it most helpful to meet consistently with her Strategic Human Resources Business Partner, Tom, to work together on the assimilation process. Tom introduced the Leader Success Inventory as the tool to facilitate a comprehensive review of the business, market, culture, talent and relationships that would be in scope for Mary's success in the role. Mary was surprised at the extent of transformation that would be required to create breakthrough performance in this market. Her organization was producing solid revenues already, so it was important for Mary to understand the culture and history of the business before introducing new changes.

The analysis helped her to see that creating a culture of aspirational thinking would be needed to achieve greater, long-term success. In the short-term, using the tools to set immediate priorities for learning, and creating the vision for the desired culture in Western Michigan, were most beneficial to Mary.

Tom, certified as an assimilation coach by the authors of The Ascending Leader, leveraged Mary's vision to serve as a partner in the drive for culture change. He also supported Mary in developing her talented team to be ready for the challenges ahead in their market.

Mary describes her approach as leading to inspire a "culture of possibility thinking" in order to achieve and sustain a breakthrough in performance!

****

Tool #3: Quick Culture Assessment

Whether you are newly promoted and/or new to the organization, the Quick Culture Assessment will help you assess, learn and adapt to the current culture of the organization. This will provide you with the foundation to lead the culture in a positive way (while honoring and preserving what works) to achieve higher performance and sustained results.

What is it?

A tool to help you consider all elements associated with successfully adapting to and potentially changing the culture in a positive way. It encompasses observable and non-observable elements including:

- Past: history, shared experiences, and context for the current vision and mission.
- Present: current beliefs and assumptions that reflect deeply held values.
- Future: desired mindsets and behaviors that will create enhanced behaviors and sustainable results.

Why use it?

To reduce the risk of being rejected!

When you are aware of and can demonstrate your appreciation for the past and present, you gain credibility quickly. This helps you to develop and to share your vision for the future with knowledge and context of the history and experiences shared by all, which will inspire others to follow. Acknowledging the successes of the past is a key strategy to begin to build influence for the future.

How to make the most of it?

1. Make notes of all you have learned in the first 30–60 days from the LS Inventory, and share with others to validate understanding.
   - o Be open about what you don't understand and be willing to learn about the past.
2. Discuss culture insights with your Manager — seek answers, input, support, and advice.
   - o Remember it is up to you to adapt and then create change as needed.
3. Clarify your own culture insights to strengthen your relationships and contribute to your vision. Gather insights from your team, peers and other stakeholders.
   - o Past: What are successes and shared experiences that you can highlight and build upon?
   - o Present: What current values should be carried forward to create continuity and honor the team?
   - o Future: What behaviors and mindsets are needed for success on the path ahead?

Quick Culture Assessment

Past: History and experience that provide context for the organization's vision and mission			
Observable – communication, norms, language, rituals, clothing and hot topics	Favorable:	Unfavorable:	Compared to previous culture:
Non-Observable – unconscious, mindsets, taken-for-granted beliefs, assumptions, perceptions and feelings	Favorable:	Unfavorable:	Compared to previous culture:

Present: Current beliefs and assumptions that indicate the organization's values			
Observable – communication, norms, language, rituals, clothing and hot topics	Favorable:	Unfavorable:	Compared to previous culture:
Non-Observable – unconscious, mindsets, taken-for-granted beliefs, assumptions, perceptions and feelings	Favorable:	Unfavorable:	Compared to previous culture:

Future: Desired mindsets and behaviors that will create improved and sustainable results			
Observable – communication, norms, language, rituals, clothing and hot topics	Favorable:	Unfavorable:	Compared to previous culture:
Non-Observable – unconscious, mindsets, taken-for-granted beliefs, assumptions, perceptions and feelings	Favorable:	Unfavorable:	Compared to previous culture:

Chapter Summary

Honor the Culture!

- Recognize the need to adapt and fit into your new environment.
- Review all aspects of the organization system and build relationships with culture influencers as a foundation for understanding the culture.
- Respect and honor the history and experiences of the team that came before you.
- Understand and highlight the current cultural values that can be leveraged for greater success.
- Gain clarity about the mindsets and behaviors needed that will be essential to future success.

Having strongly grounded yourself in your new organization's culture, you are ready to work with the system to implement your goals and ideas. To do this, however, you must build and maintain a strong connection with your manager. It is not an automatic connection; it requires concerted effort. You will benefit greatly from proactively gaining the support and advocacy you need from your manager to succeed. In the next chapter, we'll look at this critical relationship.

~Chapter 4~

Getting to Know My Boss

A few weekends later, as Pete and Annie pulled into their driveway after some errands, they saw Max sitting in his car, fully engaged with something they couldn't make out. Curious, they wandered over and asked if everything was OK.

"Sure," said Max. *"I'm just fiddling with my car's GPS. I might need it to get around my new town."*

As usual, Max asked Pete how it was going with his new promotion. Before Pete could answer, Annie blurted out, *"Pete is having a few problems with his new boss."* She made *"air quotes"* as she said problems.

Instantly annoyed, Pete snapped, *"Listen, sure I'm a VP now but I'm also new to my role and could use a little direction and support from time to time."*

He looked to Max for support, but his neighbor just listened and gave a little shrug. Pete took it for a non-verbal *"So?"* and he continued.

"I thought I'd caught a break with this woman for my boss. She's a very competent leader at the company, a real visionary, but she's involved in a slew of projects and getting five minutes with her is a real challenge."

Again, Max listened intently until it seemed Pete had gotten it all out of his system. He paused a moment longer and asked, *"How do her other VPs get time with her? Do they stop her in the hall or do they schedule appointments with her?"*

Pete shook his head and allowed that so far he has just tried to stop her as they happened to pass from time to time during the day.

Max said, *"When I got my promotion to your level, I remember running into the same kind of problem. My wife suggested that I try what helps in a lot of marriages — more communication."*

Annie laughed, *"You go, Max."*

Max grinned, and then said, *"I made an appointment on my boss's calendar. When we met I shared what I was going though, asked questions and learned a few things. We set up a series of meetings and I walked away feeling that if I played my cards right, my boss would be a critical resource."* Max held up his new GPS, *"Like this little gadget...good info 'in' gets me good directions 'out.'"*

Annie and Pete were amused by his response but kept it to themselves and left with pleasant good-byes and *"see you soons."* On the way back home Annie mused out loud, *"Interesting; use your boss as a GPS."*

Pete chuckled, *"He always has some strange advice like that with these strange analogies. But then I think about it a while, and it turns out to be pretty darn smart. His last name is Jamison? I have to Google him. He seems to have had a bunch of fairly high-level jobs."* Pete walked into their house still shaking his head over Max's latest bit of advice. *"My boss is like a GPS...."*

✳✳✳✳

Key Questions

- Have you established a good working relationship with your manager?
- Do you fully understand your manager's expectations of you?
- What can you do to proactively ensure that you and your manager are "on the same page?"
- What has worked for you in the past? What hasn't worked?
- What do you need to accomplish in the first six months and by one year to have your manager thrilled he or she hired you?

Who hasn't suffered under a bad boss from time to time? Boss bashing at the water cooler is an old tradition, now gone online thanks to Facebook. But it shouldn't be that way. Not proactively establishing an effective working relationship with your manager can result in unclear expectations, marginal support and guidance, lack of access to resources, poor communication and limited connection to key stakeholders of your success.

Impact to You: You may be unknowingly operating outside your manager's expectations, putting you at risk for failure.

- " ...Why didn't he/she tell me what the expectations were up-front?!"
- " ...How am I supposed to get that done without the resources?!"
- " ...He/she is never around!!"

Such are the laments of the leaders who happily begin a new role, only to find that they've gotten off on the wrong foot with their manager.

It's impossible to overstate the critical importance of developing an effective relationship with your manager! In fact, research from Gallup as well as Development Dimensions International (DDI), suggests that approximately 70% of an employee's satisfaction on the job (and whether or not they leave the company) is tied to this relationship.

Yet, managers these days are SO BUSY that they can neglect their leadership responsibilities — building solid relationships with their direct reports and ensuring clear expectations. Most managers don't even realize the lack of connection is happening, and they certainly don't wish it to happen; they simply go about their overwhelming myriad of meetings and responsibilities, heads down, getting the job done. When they do look up, often they realize time has passed and the new leader is not achieving at the rate expected. So, as a new leader, how do you get what you need?

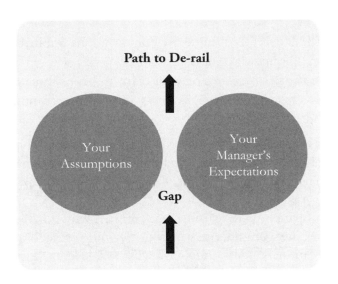

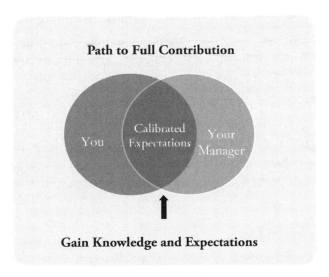

What to do? Take responsibility for your own success and ensure that you and your manager have established a good working relationship. This includes clearly aligning expectations, resources and support needs.

Top Five Strategies To Conquer This Enemy:

It will be helpful to frame the conversations outlined in the Manager Discussion Guide around how you will get results, enhance the performance of your team and contribute to your manager's success — faster! Your goal is to get the commitment you need to succeed.

1. Insist on regular meetings: you deserve the time and attention to learn at an accelerated rate to fully contribute.
2. Adapt to your manager's style preferences: don't expect your manager to adapt to you.
3. Negotiate time to learn before you perform: don't let your credibility get undermined by not gaining an accurate operational understanding of what you lead.
4. Seek clarity until you have expectations confirmed: have a no-tolerance policy for vague expectations; vague expectations yield unfocused results!
5. Support your manager's success and he or she will advocate for you: even though you have a lot to prove, being self-centered won't resonate with your boss!

It is up to the new leader to proactively seek the knowledge and understanding needed to meet expectations. In addition to meeting expectations, it is essential for a leader in a new role to establish proactive communication and a meeting rhythm to support success.

Client's Story: Dave

Every new leader has the responsibility to figure out how to be successful working with a new Manager.

Given all the demands of the role, it was natural for Dave, a new Clinical Director in a large healthcare system, to spend his time focused on the team, key stakeholders, patients, building relationships with peers and understanding the organization and culture in the context of his new team. As a newly promoted leader within an existing organization, Dave also had the added responsibility of assimilating with a team in an expanded role that would require him to build collaboration on a leadership team with physician and nursing leaders.

Dave was engaged in regular meetings with his Manager from the start, which was certainly helpful in terms of understanding the strategic and operational focus for his role. It helped Dave to hear his Manager's vision for the future and to understand the operational execution it would require from her perspective. It was not until problems began to arise that Dave recognized the need to calibrate more effectively with his Manager. He had not confirmed their working relationship to include: her preferred method for communication, how decisions would be made, the frequency or content that would be most helpful to provide in regular updates and how urgent requests would be handled. So when urgent situations occurred, each time it was stressful for Dave, not knowing exactly how to engage his Manager. He also learned through direct feedback that his Manager preferred to receive proactive communication rather than in the moment of crisis or after the situation had been resolved.

Dave utilized a regular update session to have a dedicated conversation with his Manager about calibrating their work together optimally that included: confirming how his team would fit into the vision, how they would work together, the results that needed to be achieved, the most important relationships for Dave to cultivate, and the support he could expect from his Manager.

Since the meeting, Dave has been communicating in a manner that has allowed his Manager to provide optimal support, and his relationship with her is on much more solid ground. Dave also found that when contacted proactively, his Manager often provided strategic insight about options to consider that he may not have explored on his own. Each time he managed an urgent situation and focused on proactive communication with his Manager, his confidence grew in the role.

****

The Manager Discussion Guide is a terrific tool to establish alignment with your manager and build a solid working relationship.

"The most significant challenge, really, for a new Clinical Director is to understand the hospital vision, our vision in the Patient Services Division and to be able to align his or her team to achieve it. With regular updates it is also important to help a new Clinical Director to understand my expectations, grasp how to effectively communicate and make decisions and to provide optimal patient and family experiences.

"The conversation with a new Clinical Director often begins with the operational needs such as: understanding my expectations, how best to communicate, how decisions are made and how to establish an operating rhythm. My intent for each new Director is more strategic and includes understanding the hospital and Patient Services vision as well as how to create alignment with his/her own team to achieve the vision. The investment in time, conversation and availability is well worth the effort when leaders contribute fully!"

—Becky Baute,
Assistant Vice President of Patient Services,
Cincinnati Children's Hospital

Tool #4: Manager Discussion Guide

The Manager Discussion Guide provides a structured approach to assuring alignment and a constructive working relationship.

What is it?

A tool to guide your discussions, helping you quickly align with your manager, so that you are: working well together, confirming expectations, ensuring you have the support needed and building effective relationships.

Why use it?

It assures you have effectively calibrated with your manager to be successful in your role.

How to make the most of it?

- Review the tool yourself first and think about what is most important — in the business, to your manager and for you to learn and contribute.
- Prioritize questions to ask based on importance now versus later.
- Set regular meeting times with your manager to complete these discussions.
- Identify action steps and implement them after each discussion.
- Be sure to have "course adjustment" conversations, when/if needed!

Manager Discussion Guide

Working Together		Achieving Results
How can we have the most beneficial working relationship?		What is your vision for success in six months, in one year? How will success be measured?
What is the best way for me to communicate with you? Frequency? Method?		What do I need to be focused on in order to achieve success?
What decisions do you want to be involved in?		What am I expected to achieve in the first six months? First year?
What information and communication do you prefer from me? In what frequency and format?		What would you suggest as "quick wins?"
Key Insights and Action Items		**Key Insights and Action Items**

Providing Support		Building Relationships
What should I know about the current situation?		What relationships require my immediate attention?
What resources are within my purview or otherwise accessible to me (financial, personnel, equipment, etc.)?		What relationships are essential to my success in the first six months? One year?
What authority do I have to align resources / systems?		What insights or feedback can you provide to guide me in relationship development?
To what degree will you be present and available to support me in my role?		How can I support your success?
Key Insights and Action Items		Key Insights and Action Items

Chapter Summary

Early On, Establish A Positive, Strategic Relationship With Your Manager

- Build rapport and establish a connection along with a workable operating rhythm that keeps you on track for success.
- Clarify expected results — things that you will have to accomplish in the first 6 months and 1 year that make him/her thrilled with the decision to hire you.
- Understand your level of authority and decision-making, as well as the resources and support you will have available to accomplish initiatives.

You've taken steps to calibrate with your manager to get the resources and support you need to succeed. Taking these critical steps will save you from stepping off the management cliff. In addition to building a strong working relationship with your manager, building strong relationships with other stakeholders and peers who are important to your success is also a critical step. In the next chapter, we'll look at how to identify, nurture and build good working relationships with them.

~Chapter 5~

Making Connections

Several weeks later, Pete was working in his backyard trying to trim tree branches away from the house. As he was standing on a step ladder stretching to reach a branch, he started to teeter and came dangerously close to losing his balance. Frustrated, he looked around and spied Max coming out his back door. He called the older man over and explained the problem. Max was only too happy to hold the ladder while Pete reached up and lopped off the offending branches.

"Thanks, Max. I didn't want to fall," he said.

"Glad to help, Pete. All good at work?" asked Max.

Pete considered this. He'd grown to respect Max's advice. Heck, everything Max suggested so far had pointed Pete in the right direction.

"Yes and no," said Pete as he came down the ladder. *"I got my new idea approved, so that's good, but I'm getting the feeling some people are looking at me as if I'm a cowboy or a maverick or something and that's not the real me. I mean, sure I want to impress my boss and her bosses; that's how you're supposed to get ahead in business."*

Max took a seat on the ground and Pete flopped down beside him.

"Did you ever read the poem "No Man is an Island," Pete?"

"Years ago, John Donne wasn't it?" Pete asked, *"Why?"*

"Yes, that's it. Well, when I was promoted to division president of a good-sized bank, my new boss had me read it out loud and then we talked about it. See, just as you realized you couldn't get those high branches by yourself just now, I realized that I couldn't accomplish things in my new job without good relationships with my peers and support groups."

Pete nodded as Max continued. *"They're as important to your success as your bosses are. They're your 'ad hoc' teachers; your moral support, your creative stimuli, the oil that helps you get things done faster and easier."*

Pete added, *"Not to mention that their input to my boss about me is extremely important to my future career mobility, eh?"*

Max nodded seriously, *"There's that side to it, too, Pete. The best advice my new boss ever gave me was, 'Get to really know your peers and strategic relationships and don't be afraid to ask for a bit of help.'"*

Pete thanked Max for his help with the trimming and for his advice. As he put away the ladder, he chuckled and reminded himself yet again to Google Max sometime during the next week. But then he got pretty busy.

Key Questions:

- Besides your manager and your team, who are the people that matter most to your success, in the new role and beyond?
- What have you done to build solid working relationships with internal and external stakeholders?
- Who has influence and sway in the organization?
- How can you best build connections and credibility with them?

In their desire to contribute quickly, leaders of all levels tend to overlook the relationships that will be integral to their success. Peers often have great insights about the leader's manager and how to get along in a new culture, while Stakeholders often hold the keys to successfully influence across the enterprise and beyond.

Impact to You: Failure to address this potential threat can cause those who matter most to your future success to: a.) get the wrong impression about you, b.) make faulty assumptions, and c.) contribute to your derailment.

First impressions matter!

> "People do not care how much you know until they know how much you care."
>
> — John Maxwell

... Yet all too often, intelligent, well-meaning leaders flounder in their new roles because they fail to recognize:

• The influence stakeholders have on their short-term goals and long-term career mobility.
• Who has power in the organization, including those with formal and informal influence.
• The focused attention needed early to build these relationships.
• The value of stakeholders, such as helping a leader to develop a compelling vision, garnering support for achieving it, and creating a network of relationships as a foundation for success.

So, how do you know who has the power?!

• Who are the known strategic leaders? These individuals clearly articulate and influence with a vision.
• Who has a strong network of advocates? These folks cultivate relationships, and know they are the currency of success.

- Who are the known and respected influencers? These leaders are persuasive and influence with purpose and passion.
- Who is known for strong execution? These people understand that talent is ultimately defined by consistent performance.
- Who is "in the know"? They add value by not only solving operational problems, but by helping to set the strategic agenda for the *organization*.

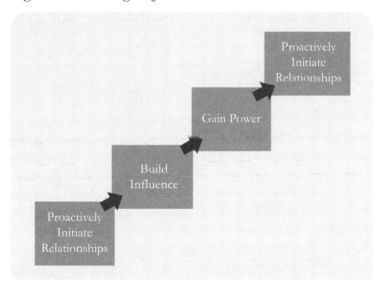

While there are a number of definitions of stakeholder, we'll use a modification of the Encarta Learners' Dictionary, which defines a stakeholder as: "somebody who benefits if something succeeds." We are encouraging you to think about who will benefit from your team's success and who can help maximize your effectiveness. Who has an interest in your success? Certainly your manager and your team, but who else? What other enterprise leaders benefit from the work your team, department or function does? Who can help you succeed? Who could get in the way of your progress?

This strategy applies whether you are new to the organization or not. Those new to the organization are particularly vulnerable, given the rush of high expectations, new learning and lack of cultural and political knowledge or understanding. But getting an internal promotion is certainly no guarantee, even if you already have a great network ... you are in a new role now, and new roles require a reassessment of stakeholders.

In the early going of any new relationship, people are making assessments and judgments about each other. Like it or not, it's the way things are. It is helpful to be both selfish and selfless at the same time (i.e., seek what you need to be successful, while offering your time and resources to help others succeed). This approach contributes to developing collaborative, trusting relationships.

Trust is crucial, and there is no better time than now to build it. When have you worked for a leader who was out for themselves? What impact did that have on you? As you know, true leadership occurs in service of others.

Strategies that Work:

1. Be humble. When you don't know much about the role it allows others to help you learn. Be willing to listen and learn and show your appreciation for stakeholder and peer contributions.
2. With the help of your manager and team, identify those who matter most to your success (besides those on your team, covered in Chapter 6). Schedule time to begin to build strong working relationships with them. The following tools will help:
   o Stakeholder Assessment (see Tool #5a)
   o Peer Discussion Guide (see Tool #5b)

3. Again, with help, consider political implications. Think about the organization as a system and understand the impact of your contribution on others across the enterprise.
4. Recognize that initial conversations and rapport are just the beginning; what you do after that is what really matters.
   o Model high character (i.e., communicate openly, maintain confidentiality, act with integrity).
   o Support and develop others (i.e., understand others' needs and contribute to success).
   o Be a servant leader (i.e., act in the best interest of others).
   o Have a high Do/Say ratio (i.e., do what you say you will do).
   o Model transparency (i.e., be okay with your imperfections and seek feedback to grow).

"Relational skills are the most important abilities in leadership."

— John Maxwell

Client's Story: Jim

Jim was a highly successful and experienced marketing executive. He first worked his way up the corporate ladder in consumer package goods Brand Management positions, then leveraged this experience to become Vice President of Marketing at a manufacturer of children's products and later General Manager of a sporting goods company.

While this was a satisfying career and one that kept his keen intellect challenged, he came to realize that as he rose in the ranks he got further and further away from what he loved: the creative process. While the management nature of the roles, the money and the prestige were great, much time was spent in tasks he simply didn't care for that much. Like it or not, these promotions had led him more and more away from the "fun" part of the work, and more toward responsibilities that helped improve efficiency and effectiveness of his organization – noble things, just not where he wanted to focus the rest of his career.

After a lot of soul-searching, networking and determination, Jim landed the perfect new role as a consultant in the strategic brand/new product positioning arm of a respected advertising agency. There was so much to learn! This was a new industry for him, a new culture and an entirely different way of doing business than he was used to. To succeed, he needed to leverage relationships inside and outside the agency, including his manager (the agency's President), his clients and, very importantly, his peers.

Jim thought strategically about who the key influencers were, who was "in the know," and who could help him steer a course through this strange, stimulating new world. He identified them along with a plan for building key relationships with them. His new career began to flourish, he was getting promoted and there came a point when he was asked to become a member of the Executive Committee, in charge of all the things for which he had left the sporting goods company. He graciously declined; for he had been there, and didn't like that!

****

94

Tool #5a: Stakeholder Assessment & Strategy Plan

The Stakeholder Assessment & Strategy Plan will help you start off with a best leadership practice — building relationships that will be strategic to your future and beneficial in your current role.

What is it?

A conduit for intentionally identifying and influencing stakeholders of your success.

Why use it?

This tool will help you focus your precious time and energy in the most efficient way, while building vital relationships and ultimately helping to maximize your success. Not inconsequentially, these relationships are often those that establish bonds that span a career and, sometimes, a lifetime.

How to make the most of it?

Consider who key stakeholders are from a number of angles.

1. Include internal as well as external stakeholders, such as industry influencers, customers, vendors and suppliers.
    o Use what you have previously learned, and the relationships you have already built, as an aid.
    o Continue to aggregate knowledge and insight as you consider each element of the tool, from the identification of stakeholders to action planning.
2. Be discriminating with the tool regarding the level of current support and level of importance to your success.
    o Seek the help of your manager, team and others if/as appropriate.
3. Develop a draft, and seek additional advice and counsel from your manager prior to taking action.

4. Purposely identify what actions, if any, are appropriate to influence each stakeholder.
5. Proactively determine how to:
    o Establish rapport
    o Contribute to their success
    o Encourage stakeholders to reciprocate
6. Use your skills of observation, asking questions and listening to help identify the key needs and concerns of the individuals.
    o Consider how you can add value to stakeholders, from the perspective of your role.
7. Think through the timing of your action plan — you cannot take all actions at once, so prioritize.
8. Review and understand Tool #5b below (Peer Discussion Guide), since it is a very helpful resource for relationship building.

Stakeholder Assessment

Identify & analyze key internal and external stakeholders of success in your role.

Define stakeholders by answering the following questions:

- Who has an interest in your success?
- What other enterprise leaders benefit from the work your team, department or function does?
- Who can help you succeed?
- Who could get in the way of your progress?
- Who are the known strategic leaders?
- Who has a strong network of advocates?
- Who are the known and respected influencers?
- Who is known for strong execution?
- Who is "in the know"?

Stakeholder Assessment

Stakeholder (Names of Individuals)	Level of Current Support (High, Med, Low)	Importance to My Success (High, Med, Low)	Take Action to Influence? (Yes / No)

Stakeholder Strategy Plan

Using the list of stakeholders above, identify those who require detailed action plans to influence.

Stakeholders Who Need to Be Influenced	Key Needs or Concerns of the Individual	Action Plans		
		What?	By Whom?	By When?

Tool #5b: Peer Discussion Guide

The Peer Discussion Guide is your resource for quickly establishing rapport and building relationships with peers and other key stakeholders.

What is it?

A strategic guide for having powerful, trust-developing conversations that contribute to rapid rapport, enhanced knowledge, better collaboration and organizational insights.

Why use it?

- Get off on the right foot with, and begin to build trust with, those who you identify as having an impact on your success.
- Learn about their roles, goals and priorities, and discuss how to optimally work together.
- Gain "insider" knowledge about how you can be successful, and how to avoid missteps.

How to make the most of it?

- Prioritize who to have these in-depth conversations with.
- Prior to meeting, identify which questions are most appropriate and most important for a given interaction.
- Pay attention! Amaze yourself with your listening skills.
- Recognize that initial conversations and rapport are just the beginning; what you do after that is what really matters. Strong relationships grow with time and are demonstrated through action.
    o It can help to take notes for future reference, and refer to them prior to other interactions.
- If you identify follow-up actions during the conversation, then follow up — your credibility depends on it!! Discuss insights with your manager; seek additional perspective.
- Identify key take-aways:

o What is most important to this person? How can I help?
o How can we work best together?
o What advice do I need/want to heed?
o What actions can I take?

Peer Discussion Guide

Area of focus	Ask Now?	Questions	Action Plans
Role Discussion	——	What are your roles and responsibilities? How do they relate to my role?	
	——	Is there anything not working well?	
	——	What insights do you have about the organization/culture that would help me to be successful in my role?	
Collaboration Discussion	——	How can I support you to achieve your goals?	
	——	What goals do we have in common from your perspective?	
	——	What are you most proud of that your organization achieved over the past year?	

Area of focus	Ask Now?	Questions	Action Plans
Organization Discussion	—	What advice do you have for being successful in this organization?	
	—	What mistakes should I avoid?	
Resources Discussion	—	Are you in need of resources from my team to be successful?	
	—	What resources should we share?	
	—	How will we work collaboratively to optimally utilize resources?	
Relationship Discussion	—	How frequently should we meet / discuss our mutual interests?	
	—	What relationships are essential to my team's success?	
	—	What relationships are strategic for me to develop?	

Chapter Summary

Building upon the work you did previously, to connect and align goals with your manager, now you've assessed your stakeholder relationships, which should now give you a broad view of most of the people who are critical to supporting your success. As we defined it, these are people who will also benefit from your success. A good deal of your efforts will need to go toward keeping these working relationships strong. Likewise, the relationship you have with your team members, those who report to you, will need attention and nurturing. For many of them, your transition into the leadership role may be stressful or a cause to celebrate; either way, it is a change that must be acknowledged and managed effectively. You will learn in the next chapter how to go about figuring out how to do just that.

~ Chapter 6 ~

Leading My Team

A short time later, on a crisp fall Saturday afternoon, Pete heard a knock at his back door. He got up from watching a college football game to see who was there.

"Hi, neighbor," said Max. *"I'm working on a leak under my kitchen sink and need a large crescent wrench. Do you have one I can borrow?"*

"Sure, come on in. I'm just watching a game," replied Pete.

"Ah," said Max, looking at the TV and seeing the score. *"My brilliant alma mater is getting clobbered again. You know for a bunch of smart people they never seem to be able to pull together as one."*

"Sounds a lot like my group," griped Pete. *"They're all really good at what they do, but getting them to work together is like trying to get horses to harmonize."*

Max laughed. *"Well, if there's one thing I learned when they made me Group Director of Mortgage Banking, it's that having smart people doesn't necessarily mean you'll have a good team."*

At this point in their relationship, Pete was a believer and asked Max to tell him about it. Max admitted it wasn't only the team members to blame.

"A large part of it was my fault as well. I was so busy trying to impress my new bosses, I didn't pay enough attention to my team members day to day...you know... listen to their concerns, get to know their styles. I also kind of down-played their earlier accomplishments, preferring to think that their real history started when I got there."

Pete realized that without knowing it, Max could have been talking about his own situation, so he asked, *"What happened?"*

"Well, I got lucky. I had lunch with an old friend who had left my group just before I took over. She gave me some background and advice that let me see I was leading without anyone following because I was so anxious to impress everyone around me."

"What was her advice?" Pete asked.

"She said that I needed to understand and value the team's history. That I should make time to understand each individual member's style and strengths and use them to create a team stronger than any one or two of us alone. She showed me that people will support what they help to create."

Max stayed awhile, drank a beer and together he and Pete watched Max's school get walloped. Then Max thanked Pete for his wrench and headed home. Pete was already thinking about how he might change a few things at work. Then he made a beeline for his computer, pulled up Google and started hunting. *"So,"* he smiled, *"Stanford University ... killer clue!"*

Key Questions:

- Have you taken the time to get to know each team member and to clarify expectations?
- Have you begun to assess the talent on your team?
- What behaviors have you exhibited in the past that could alienate your team? How can you ensure they do not recur?
- Have you given the team the opportunity to get to know you?
- What are the barriers to high performance, from the team's perspective?

The early-going for the new leader of a team is an opportunity to get off to a great start. Hopefully you have experienced that, as we have, and have benefitted from the role modeling that leaders demonstrate. When it happens (and typically it was no accident), the energy and dynamics of the team can be leveraged to accomplish wonderful things. Unfortunately, though, whether it is the overwhelm of the new role, the desire to impress their manager, other senior leaders, or coming off as arrogant and dictatorial, too often leaders in a new role alienate the direct reporting team that is now pivotal to their success.

Impact to You: Sub-optimized team results and relationships. Put yourself into the shoes of your direct reports/team members; think about the times in your career when you have reported to a new leader. What did you think? How did you feel? Typically, there is some level of anxiety. What is he/she like? What is his/her style of managing? Will we get along? Will he/she come in and change everything?!

> *"When it comes to actions that can support both enablement and energy, few things can have as much immediate impact as an effective relationship with one's direct manager."*
> — Towers Watson,
> 2012 Global Workforce Study

Developing trust as a new leader with a team is more critical and more challenging than ever before. Team members trust (or don't) based on personal style, previous team and leader experiences, as well as the business environment overall. Sadly, all too often, experience can be brutal....

The 2008 Towers Watson Global Workforce Survey showed:

- Only 49% of employees believe senior leaders act consistently with the company's values.
- Only 38% say senior leaders have a sincere interest in their well being.
- Only 38% say senior leadership communicates openly and honestly.
- Just 44% agree that senior leaders try to be visible and accessible.

Four transition pitfalls to avoid when building team engagement:

1. Neglecting your team members, whether that means being consumed by meetings or being overwhelmed by the amount of work and not attentive to their needs.
    o When you allow yourself to be consumed by meetings, your schedule is managing *you*, and your team members suffer as a result. Meet with your manager and seek support.
    o When you fail to give your team the time and attention to clarify roles and expectations, they are less engaged and productive.
    o When you bury yourself in your office to get work done, you may not be prioritizing what is most important, delegating or advocating for resources. Your time dedicated to the team is vital to your success — and theirs.
2. Changing too much too soon, whether you initiate it or are pressured to do so.
    o If you don't take the time to learn about the inner

workings of the area, including its priorities, projects, and people, yet charge ahead with your ideas, plans and actions — don't be surprised by the backlash!

o When you don't stand up to your leaders and allow them to make decisions that affect your team — know that this will erode the team's trust in you.

3. Failing to learn about and to recognize the work that has been done.

o Believe it or not, typically, decent work really was being done before you arrived; seek it out and recognize it.

o Accept what you don't know and take this narrow window of time to learn about the organization. Your credibility depends on it!

4. Sub-optimizing your team's performance by failing to assess the current performance, skill and motivation of each team member and taking action.

o Provide coaching and feedback as appropriate and ensure that the right person is in the right role.

o Often a qualified Human Resources partner can assist you in this process and will have history and context that is relevant.

In Scott Allen and Mitchell Kusy's book, *The Little Book of Leadership Development*, they point out that research indicates

> "Outstanding leaders go out of the way to boost the self-esteem of their personnel. If people believe in themselves, it's amazing what they can accomplish."
> — Sam Walton

leaders who set clearly defined expectations and agreed-on levels of performance are more likely to get positive results than leaders who don't. This is a great resource for leaders and offers fifty strategies in all by Allen and Kusy. Especially beneficial are the best practices that relate to those transitioning into new roles.

So, what to do? As noted below, the 2012 Towers Watson Global Workforce Study named five drivers of sustainable engagement that are consistent worldwide.

The Top Five Drivers of Sustainable Engagement

Priority Areas of Focus	Behaviors and Actions that Matter to Employees
1. Leadership	• Is effective at growing the business. • Shows sincere interest in employees' well being. • Behaves consistently with the organization's core values. • Earns employees' trust and confidence.
2. Stress, balance and workload	• Manageable stress levels at work. • A healthy balance between work and personal life. • Enough employees in the group to do the job right. • Flexible work arrangements.

3. Goals and objectives	• Employees understand:
	  o The organization's business goals.
	  o Steps they need to take to reach those goals.
	  o How their job contributes to achieving goals.

4. Supervisors	• Assign tasks suited to employees' skills. • Act in ways consistent with their words. • Coach employees to improve performance. • Treat employees with respect.
5. Organization's Image	• Highly regarded by the general public. • Displays honesty and integrity in business activities.

There are numerous tools and resources to help you meet the needs of your followers. The Gallop research shared in the recent book *Strengths Based Leadership*, by Tom Rath and Barry Conchie, indicates that more than 10,000 followers were interviewed to define four basic follower's needs: trust, compassion, stability and hope. When considering development options that will be most engaging for your new team, keep in mind that a consistent, ten-minute ice-breaker at the beginning of a team meeting can be effective; dedicated team-building sessions that may include a facilitator can be beneficial as well. Your team will know what is important to you based on how you focus your attention.

Client's Story: Lee Ann

Lee Ann was recently promoted into a new and important role as Director of Organizational Development and Learning. It was a new role, but not a new organization. She is a high achiever, and a reflective planner who builds great relationships with her teams.

With an external partner, Lee Ann planned and held a Team Assimilation meeting to help calibrate effectively with her new Team. A few weeks before the Team Assimilation session, she proactively met with each team member to build rapport and discuss current role, responsibilities, questions, requests and aspirations. Lee Ann knew that developing the basis of a one-on-one relationship with each member would serve her well over the next several months as well as in the long term. Going forward, Lee Ann will be assessing the needs of the business, the structure for her organization and how to assure the fit of her current Team in roles that best serve the needs of the organization.

The first half of the Team Assimilation meeting was dedicated to the Team's getting to know Lee Ann as its new leader. The second half focused on the Team providing input to Lee Ann's draft vision for the Organizational Development and Learning organization.

The first half of the meeting: *The Team had previously reported to an energetic, informal, visionary leader. They were attached to the previous leader and articulated the sense of loss they were experiencing. Lee Ann was able to listen attentively to the team's confusion with the differences in leadership style and established new understanding about how to best work together. The Team recognized the differences in style as part of the transition. They were more willing to accept Lee Ann and begin to understand the unique strengths that she brings to the role.*

The second half of the meeting: *Lee Ann shared her vision for re-aligning OD and Learning services to be more accessible and to better meet internal client needs. The Team responded favorably to the vision with comments, ideas and questions. Lee Ann asked the Team to seek best practices to confirm or amend the new vision and to meet again. She was thrilled when the team returned with actual evidence to support her vision and enthusiasm to begin working together to make the vision a reality!*

∗∗∗∗

Two key tools can help you start off on solid ground with your team, which in turn will help you achieve results more quickly. One tool is intended to help you build strong 1-1 relationships with your team members (**Tool #6a: Team Member Discussion Guide**), and the other is to help build your relationships with the team as a whole (**Tool #6b: Team Assimilation Discussion Guide**).

Failure to establish a good working relationship early with your team can contribute to behind-the-scenes talk, suspicion, distrust, confusion and low productivity.

"So many concepts in The Ascending Leader *book resonate with my experience in supporting new leaders to succeed in our organization. The Team Assimilation process has been especially*

111

beneficial as it has enabled us to support leaders to calibrate leadership and work styles quickly, to resolve differences in perception, to clarify expectations and to position them for success leading a team. The tools are user-friendly and very helpful when used to facilitate with a team.

—Sue Wilburn
Vice President of Human Resources
East Tennessee Children's Hospital

"What chance gathers she easily scatters. A great person attracts great people and knows how to hold them together."

— Johann Wolfgang von Goethe

Tool #6a: Team Member Discussion Guide

The Team Member Discussion Guide gives you a starting point for building rapport and understanding between you and your team members.

What is it?

A tool to help you quickly build strong relationships and your understanding of the talents and contributions of team members/direct reports.

Why use it?

It serves as a starting point with each team member and provides an opportunity to build relationships, ensure early understanding of background, skills and strengths and gain insights for how to be successful. These dedicated conversations provide a road map for building productive relationships and leveraging the talents of your team to perform.

How to make the most of it?

1. Review the tool yourself first and think about what is most important at this point.
2. Prioritize which questions to ask earlier vs. later.
3. Set aside scheduled time with your team members for discussion.
4. Identify action steps and implement them after each discussion.

Team Member Discussion Guide

Area of Focus	Ask Now?	Questions	Key Insights and Action Plans
The Background & Experience Discussion	——	What led you to your current role? What path did you take to get here?	
	——	Where did you grow up? Go to school? What did you study?	
	——	What would you like to share with me about your family? What do you like to do outside of work?	
The Role Discussion	——	How would you describe your roles and responsibilities? Is there anything that is unclear to you about your role?	
	——	What are your key skills and strengths?	
	——	How can I help you to be successful in your role?	
	——	What are your key goals? How can I support you to achieve them?	

Area of Focus	Ask Now?	Questions	Key Insights and Action Plans
The Relationship Discussion	——	What are you most proud of that you achieved in the past year?	
	——	How can we work together most effectively? Meetings, frequency, etc?	
	——	What other team members and people outside the team are most important to your success? How are those relationships going?	
	——	What advice do you have for me for being successful here?	
	——	What relationships are essential to our team's success? What relationships are most important for me to develop?	
The Situation Discussion	——	How would you describe the team now?	
	——	What barriers do you think need to be removed?	
	——	How will we work collaboratively to best utilize resources?	
	——	What potential pitfalls should I avoid?	

Tool #6b: Team Assimilation Meeting Guide

The Team Assimilation Meeting Guide gives your team the opportunity to get to know you better as a leader, ask questions and provide valuable input for the future.

What is it?

A tool to support the new leader in calibrating expectations and building positive relationships with the team.

Why use it?

For the team: It provides a safe and supportive environment for the team to get to know more about the leader, voice key concerns and identify priorities and actions.

For the leader: It establishes expectations, clarifies communication practices, builds rapport and provides a first opportunity to engage the team in initial dialogue about the vision.

How to make the most of it?

1. Review the tool.
2. Ideally, identify a Human Resources or external facilitator and discuss the plan for the meeting.
3. Identify a date for the session and communicate the agenda with the team.
4. Prepare for the session with the facilitator.
5. Identify pre-work that will give team members an opportunity to think about things ahead of time, and will maximize the use of time during the session.
6. Prepare yourself ahead of the session, recognizing that a key aspect of the session's success will be your approach to it, your willingness to listen and your open, honest communication.

7. Implement the session, with the aid of the facilitator if possible. (Bring the best version of yourself to the session!)
8. Review key take-aways and action items at the end of the session.
9. Recognize that you and the team need to prioritize actions; not everything can be done right away!
10. Commit to follow up with the team on action items and outstanding issues.
11. If appropriate, set up a meeting rhythm until actions are complete.
12. Acknowledge the team for their participation and willingness to participate.

Team Assimilation Meeting Guide

Purpose: Support the new leader in quickly building rapport with his/her team while getting issues and questions out on the table to be resolved.

Time: 2–3 hour meeting

	Action Steps	Timing

1.	**PRE-WORK:**
	• Have each team member and the leader come prepared with:
	• Professional background and current role
	  o Strengths
	  o Family/hobbies and interests	

2.	**INTRODUCTION and SESSION OBJECTIVES** • Provide brief introductions and an overview of the session objectives. • Leader should express their support of the process and opportunity to learn more. • Team members and leader share items from Pre-work. • Leader leaves the room.	

Action Steps	Timing

3. **QUESTIONS for DISCUSSION**
 	
    Facilitator explains to the team that they will be identifying questions that they would like the new leader to answer about himself / herself as a person and as a leader. The team will also have the opportunity to identify things they would like the leader to know about them as a team.
 	
Questions:
 	
• What do you already know about this leader?
 	
• What do you want to know about the leader as a person (professional, personal, preconceptions, rumors, etc.)?
 	
• What do you want to know about the leader as a manager (priorities, work style, norms, hot buttons, communication preferences, etc.)?
 	
• What do you want the leader to know about you as a team?
 	
    Facilitator explains to the team that they will be identifying questions that they would like the leader to answer and know. The team will also have the opportunity to identify things they would like the manager to know about them as a team.	

	Action Steps	Timing

3.	**QUESTIONS for DISCUSSION (cont.)**
	
	Questions:
	
	• What does the manager need to know to be successful in new role?
	  o What are the top three issues?
	  o What are the secrets to being effective?
	  o What ideas do you have for the leader?
	
	• What significant issues need to be addressed immediately?
	  o Are there any quick fixes that are needed now?
	  o Are there any difficult areas of the business that the leader should know about?
	
	• What insights and ideas do you have for the future vision of the team?
	
	Tip: Use flip charts to record responses	

4.	**DIALOGUE** • Leader re-joins the meeting. Facilitator walks through the questions and comments posed by the team. • Leader responds to questions and shares thoughts and comments. • If appropriate, set up follow-up meetings.	
5.	**THANK YOU AND NEXT STEPS** • Meeting thank you and next steps. • Adjourn.	

Chapter Summary

Engage Your Team!

- Investing in dedicated 1-1 team member meetings up-front pays huge dividends, both in relationships and performance. Trust builds and ultimately they will invest in your success!
- Give the team an opportunity to see you as a leader that listens, responds to things that are important to them, and will advocate on their behalf.
- You can achieve with speed when you take the time to assimilate with your team.
- Provide the opportunity for your team to provide input and contribute to the future vision and plan (*see Chapter 7*).

You have taken a deep-dive into your team's strengths and capabilities, now you can refocus your ideas into prioritized, practical initiatives. You will move ahead respecting what has happened in the past that has worked, and addressing what needs to be modified. You are ready to set plans for action, which is the focus of the next chapter.

~ Chapter 7 ~

Creating a Plan

After the football game, Pete finally looked up Max's career history and, quite frankly, was amazed that he'd been receiving career advice from someone with such a stellar business pedigree. Early the following week, Pete decided to seek Max out for a chat. He had no vexing problem this time; he'd just grown to truly enjoy Max and their discussions. There was no doubt finding Max's story on the web made the friendship even more special for him. Kind of like living next to Michael Jordan, he thought with a smile, but a business Michael Jordan.

He found Max out in his backyard measuring and staking string all over the place. He watched quietly for a while, and began to see forms taking shape. Finally he asked Max what he was doing.

"Laying out our dream backyard," replied Max. *"Hey, don't fall in. This is our new swimming pool. And over there is my wife's rose garden. In the back there, nestled under the elms will be our gazebo, wired for music and lighting with retractable screens if it gets too buggy."*

"Why don't you just hire someone to do all this for you?" asked Pete.

"I did so much delegating and empowering in my career, I guess I'm trying to do more for myself these

days," said Max. *"Besides, I've always been a sucker for the 'circle of accomplishment.'"*

"Circle of accomplishment?" asked Pete. *"What's that?"*

"You know, Pete, you and I have been having some interesting conversations about some of the 'enemies' you've run into as you took over your new leadership position. Fighting self-doubts and negative impulses, fighting the steep learning curve, developing a smooth relationship with a new boss, peers and team members, all very important in a leader, wouldn't you say?"

"Absolutely," Pete said with a smile, *"But why do I feel you're about to put the big bow on the gift you've been patiently giving me over the past few months?"*

Max laughed. *"Am I that transparent? Well, yes, there is a leadership bow. You see all this string and the different shapes it's taking?"*

"I do," said Pete.

"These shapes are the result of years of talks and dreaming with my wife about how we'd like our retirement home to be. Not just another 'McMansion' cut out of someone else's imagination, but one from our own vision of what our home would be like to make our retirement happy and enjoyable."

Pete looked around the yard, taking it all in.

"Now I'm planning that vision with string. That's what I call 'the circle of accomplishment': Have the vision, plan for its success..." Max bowed slightly and grinned. *"...And brilliantly execute the plans."*

Pete laughed and added, *"If you do say so yourself."*

"*I do, Pete,*" said Max laughing. Pete could sense a touch of the energy that must have been present all during Max's career.

"*Because without a shared vision and a plan that will inspire others to help you achieve it, you're not truly leading, are you?*"

Pete thought a moment and replied, "*No, Max. You're not. You may be working really hard, but you're not truly leading.*"

Pete looked at Max and put out his hand. "*I want you to know how much I appreciate the gifts you've given me over the last few months. They've really made a big difference.*"

Gripping Pete's hand, Max replied, "*I've enjoyed watching you grow, Pete. If I'm any judge, you're on the road to having a great impact as a leader.*"

****

> **Key Questions:**
>
> - Do you understand all aspects of the business well enough to articulate an aligned vision as a foundation for business planning?
> - How can you involve your team and other stakeholders in the articulation of the vision for the future? Remember, people will support what they help to create!
> - Have you (with the engagement of your team) developed a Business Plan that, when implemented, contributes to the achievement of the Vision?

The pressure is on for new leaders to produce immediately. So, why take the time to set a vision and plan? Lacking an effective vision and plan, a leader has missed the opportunity to build credibility in order to effectively lead and achieve results. The strategies and tools presented throughout this book are intended to help leaders quickly assimilate all the knowledge needed to craft an aligned vision and create a focused business plan.

Impact to You: Failure to articulate your Vision and Business Plan with purpose and passion may cause: a.) you to be seen as on operational versus strategic leader; b.) your team to lack direction, engagement and inspiration; c.) your Manager to question your ability to contribute and to provide leadership, and; d.) you to have low credibility with peers and key stakeholders.

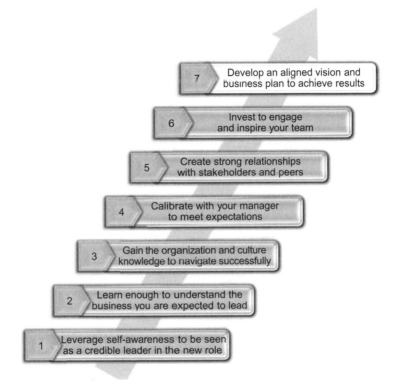

Setting direction and gaining buy-in are essential!

However, leaders often mistake the organization's vision as adequate to lead their own teams, and they underestimate the value of developing and executing a formal Business Plan.

Why articulate an aligned Vision and Business Plan?

Articulating an Aligned Vision aggregates learning gained in the new role, including: manager input, peer conversations, stakeholder discussions, team input and your own observations, insights and knowledge. The Aligned Vision serves as your team's compass. It also captures and communicates your understanding about how your responsibilities fit into the organization's vision and strategy for growth.

Developing a Business Plan includes the Aligned Vision and is the visible and tangible representation of your ability to begin to add value — as a result of your learning and all previous experience. The Business Plan serves as a road map to focus your team on the right priorities and to achieve results in the business, creating the vehicle to gain buy-in from your manager, key stakeholders and team.

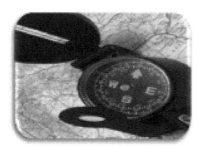

"Go to the people. Learn from them. Live with them. Start with what they know. Build with what they have. The best of leaders when the job is done, when the task is accomplished, the people will say we have done it ourselves."

— Lao Tzu

In the first 90 to 120 days you will need to assimilate a tremendous amount of information about the organization, culture, business environment, customers, history of performance, current state of operations as well as information from key stakeholders, peers and team members to develop an effective Aligned Vision and Business Plan.

To begin, the Aligned Vision includes:

1. The Organization Vision and Strategy.
2. Aligned Vision elements that link to the organization strategy and are most relevant to your area of responsibility.
3. Results that are expected in the next year.
4. Constraints or barriers that will need to be overcome.
5. Mindsets or new ways of thinking needed in order to be successful.
6. Actions including specific new behaviors that will need to be adopted to achieve results.

What are some of the traps leaders can fall into when preparing and creating an Aligned Vision?

- Lack of complete understanding of the organization strategy, business environment and customer drivers, which can minimize the opportunity to align with a comprehensive vision.
- Poor assessment of the culture, key stakeholders and executive demands can result in an aligned vision that is insufficient to meet the real needs of the team and the business.
- Lack of clarity about business imperatives and full understanding of results expected can mitigate success of the Aligned Vision, and may cause a performance deficit.
- Ignoring the current mindsets (beliefs, values and ways of thinking) that reflect the current culture norms can cause resistance to the vision that is difficult to overcome.
- Failure to articulate a clear set of actions that give the team direction can result in limited progress.

Strategies that Work:

1. Seek input in all relationships prior to creating the Aligned Vision and Business Plan.
2. Engage your team to complete the Aligned Vision Worksheet as a foundation for development of the Business Plan. (See Tool #7a: Aligned Vision Worksheet)
3. Test drive the initial draft of the Aligned Vision with your manager and peers prior to creating the Business Plan.
4. Use all elements of the Aligned Vision to develop your Business Plan.(See Tool #7b: Business Plan)
5. Once complete, develop a consistent communication message about your vision and plan and share it to build credibility and gain buy-in to your vision.

So, what happens when you have successfully created an Aligned Vision and Business Plan with the input of your manager, stakeholders, peers and team? It helps you to rapidly build credibility as a strategic leader and ensures that relationships are being nurtured in the process. Additionally you are focused on the right goals to drive the business to achieve high performance at an accelerated rate.

Client's Story: Tom

In late 2011, Tom was named President of his organization's Carolinas region and was excited about the opportunities the promotion presented. A 22-year veteran of the company and a proven leader, he wondered how the new "Leader Assimilation Program" (that his Human Resources Business Partner, Regina, encouraged him to pursue) could benefit him. Despite that bit of doubt, and after a sluggish start to the process, one Saturday morning he was determined to give it his earnest attention and sat down at the desk in his home office to do just that.

To Tom's surprise and ultimate delight, the tools he reviewed and worked with seemed to shed a new and different light on the business he was now leading. While the tools were helpful on the whole, Tom found that the one that was "absolutely most important" for him was the Aligned Vision Worksheet.

As Tom worked away that Saturday morning, he found that the time flew by and that his enthusiasm for the work to be done in the region was growing. His thoughts and notes on the Aligned Vision Worksheet helped him realize at a deeper level how he could connect and translate the organization's Vision, Purpose and Value Proposition with his region - and distinguish itself from the competition. He was creating the bridge and that was thrilling!

Moreover, he realized that the concepts of growth and profitability had more robust meanings than usual. They also applied to the people who worked within the region, and to the communities which they served. Employees and their communities would individually and collectively grow and profit from the organization's success as well.

Importantly, Tom knew he had to communicate these thoughts in a compelling way, bringing them to life for the team and fostering commitment. With Regina's help, along with the Business Plan template that incorporates strategic communication, he was able to do that with great success. In Tom's message to his employees, he stated, "Employees, customers and shareholders must know that we are the 'real deal'. They have to know by our actions that they can trust us. And we have to show by our actions that we provide something different; something of value."

With the related Business Plan, Tom and his team identified the goals, desired outcomes — including financial, community involvement, diversity, and career growth within the Carolinas — and the focused actions needed to begin to realize the vision.

One year later, Tom knows that these beginnings, powered through the year by the concerted efforts of his terrific team, contributed to a wonderfully strong year in financial results for the region. And while the vision has been tweaked and honed further, the work he did that Saturday is still the foundation for the region's future.

****

> "If your actions inspire others to dream more, learn more, do more and become more, you are a leader."
>
> — John Quincy Adams

Tool #7a: Aligned Vision Worksheet

Creating an Aligned Vision will guide your path toward full contribution as a leader. The process will help you gain credibility quickly, so buy-in to the Aligned Vision and Business Plan are possible.

What is it?

A strategic guide to:

- Reflect the organization vision, mission, values and culture.
- Align division/department/individual goals with organizational strategy.
- Inspire employees toward the pursuit of goals.

Why use it?

It provides a format and process to arrive at a comprehensive Aligned Vision.

- In order to complete it, leaders must learn about and understand the organization strategy, vision, mission, culture, goals and current results.
- It builds confidence that the right vision will lead to success, helping a leader to:
  o Gain credibility and buy in quickly.
  o Be seen as a high potential by having a strategic vision to share.

How to make the most of it?

1. Carry the document around and make notes as you have insights about what will need to be included in the Aligned Vision.
2. Engage your manager, peers, key stakeholders and team in informal dialogue about all of the elements of the Aligned Vision.
3. Seek HR support, if possible, to facilitate the Aligned Vision Worksheet session with your team, which will

encourage input and gain buy-in before the Aligned Vision is complete.

4. Use the Aligned Vision as a platform for communication and strategic influence.

Aligned Vision Worksheet

An effective aligned vision:

- Reflects organization vision, mission, values and culture.
- Aligns Division / Department / Individual vision and goals with organizational strategy.
- Inspires staff toward the pursuit of goals.

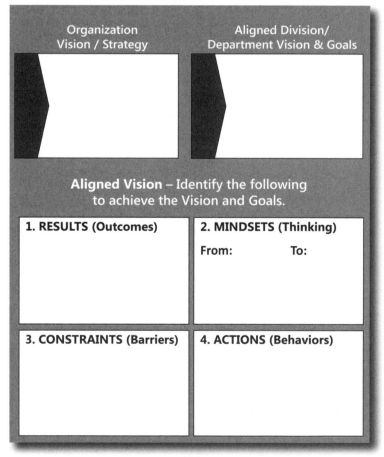

Tool #7b: Business Plan

Creating a Business Plan is the formal result of turning all the learning you have assimilated into a comprehensive plan that serves as a road map for your success and that of your team.

What is it?

A strategic plan and presentation to:

- Gather feedback on your understanding of the organization vision, mission, values and culture.
- Seek input to your aligned vision, goals, key result areas and measures for success.
- Gain executive buy-in and team commitment to the plan.

Why use it?

- It provides a formal record of your plan and executive support of the plan.
- When complete, this plan outlines the strategies and actions required to achieve annual goals that can be divided into monthly objectives, with measurement and timelines for success. A great road map!
- The approved plan ensures a leader has support for achieving results.

How to make the most of it?

1. Seek out best practices of written plans within the organization and understand fully what elements are expected in a Business Plan.
2. Engage your manager, peers, key stakeholders and team in informal dialogue about all of the elements of the Business Plan.

3. Solicit manager and team feedback before drafting the plan to ensure buy-in and that you are on path with expectations.
4. Use the Business Plan as a detailed road map for communication with executive leadership, key stakeholders, manager, peers and your team.

Your strategy to contribute fully can be realized with an effective Business Plan if you adhere to it throughout the year and update it as change dictates. Remember that your Business Plan is effective when you achieve results promised in your plan.

Business Plan

The Business Plan goals are to be aligned with Performance Management goals for the year. This Business Plan worksheet is intended to help the Leader: a.) develop plans to accomplish the goals, and; b.) present the plan to key audiences.

Aligned Vision	Strategic Communications

Goals: 6 to 12-Month Business Initiatives	
Business Results:	Employee Engagement:
Customer Engagement:	Core Values and Leadership Competencies.

Goals	Desired Outcomes	Action Item	Due Date/ Status

Chapter Summary

Articulate a Vision and Business Plan!

A well-articulated Aligned Vision and Business Plan are your opportunities to lead in a targeted, focused and influential way. The execution of these are HOW YOU GET RESULTS, which is why you are in the role to begin with!

Epilogue

Pete returned to Max's house a week or so later to invite Max over to his place the following weekend for beers and to watch the next football game.

To Max's amazement and glee, this time Stanford won. After the game, Pete went into the kitchen under the guise of getting another beer and returned with a small gift-wrapped package. Annie came in behind him.

"Annie and I wanted to thank you for all your help and advice over the last few months. Getting promoted isn't as much fun as most people think it is and you really helped me through the toughest parts."

He handed Max the package.

"You folks didn't have to do this," Max protested. *"I enjoyed every moment of listening to myself talk."*

"Oh, Max," Annie laughed.

When the wrapping was off, Max held up a frame. Within it, in calligraphic writing, was a list of some kind. Max began to read.

"Max's Maxims," he began, and then stopped and cleared his throat.

Pete stepped in, *"It's a collection of sage advice that a newly promoted leader should always keep in mind. I made them up myself."*

Annie groaned and jabbed Pete in the shoulder, *"Yeah, with a little help from your neighbor."*

Max coughed and then said in a soft voice, *"Why, it's the nicest honor I've ever gotten. I'll put it on top of my desk at home."*

He stepped over and put his arms around both his new friends' shoulders, *"I surely will."*

Annie and Pete looked at each other remembering the Google write-up on Max (aka C. Maxwell Jamison) they had found earlier in the week. They imagined their homemade plaque sitting proudly among the prestigious awards and honors garnered by Max during his amazing career. And they smiled.

(See Max's Maxims and his LinkoPedia write-up on the following pages.)

Max's Maxims

The Wisdom of C. Maxwell Jamison

◇◇◇◇◇◇◇◇◇◇◇◇◇◇◇◇◇◇◇◇◇◇◇◇◇◇◇◇◇◇◇◇◇

Have the Confidence to Conquer the Enemy Within

★

You Can't Truly Manage What You Don't Understand

★

*A Company's Culture Can Sink You If You Can't
Navigate the Waters*

★

Leverage Your Boss Like a GPS

★

*Without Your Peers and Strategic Relationships,
Success Is Impossible*

★

*Progress Happens Faster When You Listen and
Give Your Team the Chance to Contribute*

★

*Without a Vision and a Plan,
You're Not Really Leading*

★

C. Maxwell Jamison

From: LinkoPedia — the on-line encyclopedia

C. Maxwell, "Max" Jamison (born July 8, 1946) is an American financial executive. From 2001 to 2013, he was CEO (and later Chairman & CEO) of NYC National Bank & Trust, the fourth largest bank in the United States. He retired at the end of 2013. During his tenure at NYCNB&T, the bank grew from sixth largest to fourth largest and the company's value rose 600%. He is largely credited for creating early internal screening policies that kept his bank out of the sub-prime mortgage scandal that swept the nation into fiscal recession from 2008 to 2013. He was named to Fortune Magazine's Best CEO in America list every year from 2003-2013. He was named that magazine's CEO of the year in 2010.

Early Life and Education

"Max" Jamison was born in Port Washington, New York to Charles, a manufacturer's representative, and Margaret, a homemaker.

Jamison attended Chaminade High School in Mineola, New York, was awarded an athletic scholarship to Stanford University where he earned Honorable Mention as a Pac 10 quarterback and graduated *magna cum laude* in International Finance in 1965.

Jamison attended graduate school at the University of Chicago, Booth School of Business, where he earned his MBA in Accounting (1970) and his PhD in Economics (1973). During summer breaks, he worked in Manufacturers Hanover Trust's (MHT) Executive Training program back home in New York, where he first began developing relationships with senior banking executives that were to play a large part in his outstanding career.

Career

Jamison started full time at MHT after graduation in June 1973 and rose rapidly through the ranks, eventually being named Executive Vice President of International Lending (headquartered in London) where his stewardship is credited with doubling MHT's overseas revenues in just three years.

He left MHT in 1985 to become President of America's Bank & Trust (ABT), headquartered in San Francisco. Jamison tapped into the international relationships he had developed in London and, foreseeing the growth that would eventually drive Asia to the forefront of world economy, used ABT to link European interests with those of Japan and China, tripling the firm's revenue and doubling and redoubling its stock price over the course of his eight-year tenure. He was promoted to COO in 1992. He left ABT shortly after becoming COO when, in 1993, President Bill Clinton, appointed Jamison to his Council of Economic Advisors. He kept the position for six years (until 1999) and is credited with providing his economic prowess coupled with fiscal common sense as those years saw America's economy as the strongest on the globe.

During a two-year hiatus after his government service, when most ex-inner circle Washingtonians opt to write "tell-all" memoirs, Jamison chose instead to write a text book on

Banking and Finance. *Before It's Too Late* warned of the lack of oversight on Wall Street's way of doing business and the banking community's greedy pursuit of profit at all cost. He foresaw that these abuses sowed the seeds of disaster. His prophecy became reality in 2008 when speculation in real estate junk bonds snowballed into the eventual nationwide collapse of the housing market and nearly collapsed the banking industry. The textbook is still used in graduate programs today as a case study for corporate greed run amok and the proper role of government oversight.

When First Mid-America recruited him in 2001, Jamison was ready to return to work. Using the research for his book and the knowledge gleaned during his tenure in Washington, he began making changes in personnel and policy that were in place and incorporated well before the real-estate market crash in 2008.

Max Jamison was certainly well known and publicly acknowledged for his financial expertise. He is well-regarded as an expert in strong team building, excellent communication in all directions and his down-to-earth, roll-up-your-sleeves demeanor. His track record for stepping into new and difficult roles during his career made him a leader you'd want to follow.

Conclusion

All too often, we at LEI Consulting are called in to help a leader who has not transitioned well. By the time we are engaged, it is critical for the leader to improve, and sometimes it is too late to regain credibility.

It is heartbreaking to see the many missteps and mistakes that could have been avoided with the understanding and application of the concepts herein. The detrimental impact is far-reaching; the leader is typically very stressed, the leader's manager is frustrated, goals are not being reached, peers and key stakeholders are often disgruntled, and the team he or she leads may be disengaged and demoralized.

Many parents try to teach their kids as early as possible to get it right the first time when it comes to developmental skills and homework. The old adage "You only get one chance to make a good first impression" applies here as well – recovering is much more challenging than starting off strong.

Experience is a great teacher! Leaders who are most successful transitioning into new roles adopt a comprehensive approach to learning, coupled with a keen interest in nurturing relationships as a foundation for high performance. Successful transitioning leaders are humble, self-aware students of the business, organization and culture they are joining, and seek mentors to help navigate. So, investment in relationships and gaining knowledge first rather than jumping into the myriad of tasks at hand is a critical step toward success. While tasks will get checked off and new ones will come to take their place, the relationships and knowledge you develop will last a lifetime.

Our hope for you is that this knowledge, along with the tools and strategies, will contribute to your success in your current role and all future roles. There is tremendous power and influence that come with having a comprehensive Vision and Business Plan; build your credibility on these.

In all you do, seek to serve the interests of others and you can't go wrong!

To your success!

Acknowledgments

While this is certainly not the Academy Awards, we now understand why those winners exceed their time allotment for acknowledgements – there are so many people who were instrumental in the final accomplishment! Similarly, there are many people we want to acknowledge and thank for their participation, either directly or indirectly, in the discovery, development and delivery of this book.

We want to express heartfelt thanks and deep appreciation to Tom Schenck for his creativity, talent and sensitivity in bringing Pete and Max to life.

The Leadership Excelleration, Inc. (LEI Consulting) team is a dream team! We are indebted to Michelle Pennington and Amanda Blum for their professionalism, creativity and dedication to the work we do collectively, and for their commitment to helping make this book a reality. Leslie Goss brings joy and imagination to life in her work, and Matt Marvin is an esteemed colleague and contributor whose ingenuity we admire!

Our gratitude goes to the many contributors of this work, including our outstanding clients, who are such a blessing and the source of our passion to create this book. We are grateful for the opportunity to serve and appreciate the relationships with them more than we could possibly express in words. We are grateful to the many leaders at Fifth Third Bank, General Electric, Cincinnati Children's Hospital Medical Center, East Tennessee Children's Hospital, TriHealth, UC Health and so many others, who are an inspiration to us with their dedication to leaders success.

We are particularly thankful to Brent Carter, who is a role model of collaboration and partnership and whose dedication to the successful development and implementation of the Leader Assimilation Program at Fifth Third Bancorp was a cornerstone for the program's success. Our gratitude goes to Fifth Third Bancorp leadership, who are visionary leaders in this work, and to assimilating leaders and their coaches, for their skilled application of the concepts and for proving that it makes a difference. We appreciate the foresight and influence of Lauris Woolford, Greg Love, and Bonnie Newland, for their leadership and guidance of the program.

We want to express heartfelt appreciation to those who provided their stories; we are thankful for their openness in sharing their experiences, and helping other leaders by so generously sharing their experiences. Specifically, our sincere thanks to Renee, Brad, Mary, Lee Ann, and Tom!

Thank you to Scott Allen, Elizabeth (Lis) Baldock, Becky Baute, Matthew Kelly, Bonnie Newland, Sue Wilburn and Lauris Woolford, for reading the book and providing such insightful comments that will inspire our readers.

We are grateful to our strategic partners, who share our passion for helping leaders succeed. The leaders and colleagues from the University of Cincinnati (UC) Goering Center as well as the UC Center for Corporate Learning are a delight to work with.

Special thanks to Anne Schenck, for her amazingly keen eye, and to Sue Russell, for her collaborative spirit and contribution to the Stakeholder Assessment tool.

Our mentors at Xavier University, Dr. Brenda S. Levya-Gardner, Associate Professor and Director for Executive Human Resource Development Graduate Program and Dr. Sharon Korth, Associate Professor, we can't thank you enough! Your mentorship, dedication, guidance and support have been a foundation to the success of LEI Consulting.

It has been an absolute pleasure to work with the Smart Business Network team of Dustin Klein, Randy Wood, Jessica Hanna, Lori Smith, Kaelyn Hrabak, Lauren Campana and Krystal Burwell. You have made our first foray into publishing a book a true joy with your openness, flexibility, quick turn around and professionalism. Plus, you are all just so nice and enjoyable to work with!

Sam Glazer, we appreciate your enthusiasm, encouragement and coaching, and we look forward to working more with you.

We want to also thank everyone who encouraged us to make this book a reality. You were cheerleaders throughout and provided valuable feedback along the way; without you, this may never have come to fruition.

Leadership Excelleration, Inc.

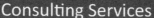

Are your leaders prepared to succeed in your organization today and ready for the challenges ahead? LEI Consulting is an excellent choice as a partner to develop the full capacity of your leadership talent.

Executive Coaching

LEI Executive Coaches have the expertise to guide executives to significantly enhance leadership effectiveness.
As a *Preferred Coaching Partner* in organizations, LEI coaches have created outstanding results. We offer your organization a strategic coaching partnership and will invest the time to learn about your business, organization, vision and culture to add value, quickly.

Leadership Development

LEI Consultants have a passion for developing leaders and have considerable expertise in leadership development that includes: leadership development program facilitation, team and executive coaching, speaking engagements, and presentations.

Organizational Effectiveness

LEI Consulting has an outstanding track record of supporting leaders to dramatically improve performance.
Organizational improvement projects include organization-wide, division and department initiatives. This assessment typically includes priorities for leadership, structure , culture, patient experience, staff satisfaction and improved performance. LEI Consulting has a *90+% success rate in current client companies.*

LEI Consulting, where every leader matters

148

Leadership Excelleration, Inc.
Leadership Assimilation

Did you know that 40% of leaders fail
within the first 18 months in a new role?
Typically, it is due to poor assimilation.

Leader Assimilation Certification

This high impact Program improves the success rate of newly hired or promoted leaders. Capturing the wisdom of best practices from more than 16 years of Executive Coaching and consulting experience, it was created to proactively address key areas that all too often are inadvertently neglected.

The Audience: Internal HR Leaders and Coaches who currently, or in the future, seek to serve as Assimilation Coaches.

Coaching Audience: New and promoted leaders within 90 days of hire or appointment.

Format: Two full day training sessions focused on each of the **seven enemies that new and promoted leaders face**, followed by Master Coaching that includes three sessions for each participant.

Content: Comprehensive Leader Success Inventory and process that includes more than 20 tools for coaches to use in each aspect of a Leader's assimilation. The Leader 's goal is to create sponsorship with his/her Manager and accelerate the process to adapt, influence and lead successfully in the new role.

Impact to the Organization:
Increased leader success in new roles, improved competitive advantage, reduced risk of turnover and associated costs, enhanced capability of leaders to fully contribute, faster in their new roles.

Leader Assimilation for Promoted Leaders

This program equips newly promoted leaders with the knowledge and skills needed to transition quickly into new roles and fully contribute.

The Audience: Newly hired, transferred or promoted leaders at all levels.

Format: One full day training session.

Content: Introduction of strategies and nine tools presented in *The Ascending Leader* book as well as a copy of the book and tools to guide individual leader success at an accelerated rate.

LEI Consulting, where every leader matters